THE QUEST FOR WANSDYKE

To
Janet, Ed and Will

East Wansdyke: view east from Morgan's Hill showing in the distance the earthwork ascending Tan Hill .

The
Quest
for
WANSDYKE

Alan Soldat

THE HOBNOB PRESS

First published in the United Kingdom in 2022

by The Hobnob Press,
8 Lock Warehouse,
Severn Road, Gloucester GL1 2GA
www.hobnobpress.co.uk

British Library Cataloguing in Publication Data
A catalogue record for this book is available from the British Library

ISBN 978-1-914407-38-3

Typeset in Scala 11/14 pt.
Typesetting and origination by John Chandler

Front cover: Aerial view of East Wansdyke looking towards Morgan's Hil (reproduced by kind permission of Historic England).

Back cover Wansdyke from Milk Hill.

Contents

Acknowledgements

This project had its gestation back in 2011. My thanks go to Roger Jones of the Ex-Libris Bookshop in Bradford on Avon who kindly read the text and recommended it to John Chandler at the Hobnob Press, so resurrecting it and setting it on the road to publication. I have not discussed the project widely, preferring to rely on synthesising a narrative from the many written sources out there. The late Bruce Eagles was kind enough to read the synopsis and offer some helpful comments, which gave me confidence that I was on the right track at a time when publication did not seem in prospect. Otherwise the contents, and the mistakes, are pretty much all my own.

The keepers of the written sources deserve a mention as they have never failed to find even what seemed like the most obscure sources: the Wiltshire Museum at Devizes, the Wiltshire and Swindon History Centre in Chippenham and the Bristol Central Library. Others have helped with illustrations, including Wiltshire Council's Archaeology Service, the Salisbury Museum, Radstock Museum and Historic England.

My Wife, Janet, helped with the photographs and clambered over more ancient earthworks than she ever knew existed.

Finally, my thanks go to John Chandler, who has guided me through the publication process effortlessly and has played a crucial role in making this a far better book than it would have been in 2011.

Alan Soldat
July 2022

I

Introduction

One of my favourite walks is on the Marlborough Downs in Wiltshire. It forms a circuit of Milk Hill, the highest point in the County, taking in the Alton Barnes White Horse, breathtaking views across the Vale of Pewsey to the south and sometimes, in the summer, there used to be a crop circle or two, although I haven't seen any lately. The walk begins with a steady climb north-westwards from the car park on the road between Alton Barnes and Lockeridge. At the top you are presented with another spectacular view, this time northwards across the Kennet Valley, one of the oldest landscapes in Britain. In the bottom of the valley stands Silbury Hill looking for all the world like a giant upturned

Wansdyke from Milk Hill

pudding bowl. This acts as a reference point to locate Avebury and West Kennet Long Barrow, which are also down there.

But then, if all this was not enough, you look to the side and you are presented with the extraordinary sight of a giant bank and ditch snaking its way across the downs as far as the eye can see. This is Wansdyke, which at this point is a spectacular monument in a spectacular landscape. Then comes the inevitable question 'what's it for?', and I realised I had no idea. It must have been a huge engineering operation for its time - but what time? It must have formed a boundary of some sort but when was this country borderland? What connection - if any - did it have with monuments like Silbury Hill and Avebury Stone Circle down in the valley below?

I was also aware that Wansdyke turns up again in the Bristol-Bath area. It gave its name to a local government district between 1974 and 1996 in the days of Avon County Council, which subsequently became part of Bath and North East Somerset District. It also gave its name to a Parliamentary constituency in the same area until 2010.

When I spoke to people about it, it became apparent how many people were not aware of Wansdyke at all, let alone what it was for, so without further ado let's explain what Wansdyke is. It is a large, long, linear bank and ditch construction, now generally acknowledged to be in two sections both running east-west: A 9 mile section runs from Maes Knoll south of Bristol to Combe Down south of Bath in the 'traditional' county of Somerset and a 12 mile long section runs from Morgan's Hill between Calne and Devizes to near Savernake Forest south of Marlborough in the county of Wiltshire, though we will look at departures from these assumptions. The ditch is on the north side of the bank from which the conclusion has been drawn that it was built by the people living on its south side - the people of what we now call Somerset and Wiltshire. We know from archaeological excavations and the examination of Saxon land charters that it could have been built any time between the Roman period and just after 900 AD. This is a completely different time horizon to Avebury and Silbury Hill, and Wansdyke clearly has nothing to do with these much earlier constructions.

So here we have a major bank and ditch construction which is comparatively little known. There are longer barrier structures in Britain, such as Offa's Dyke and Hadrian's Wall, but not many. Only

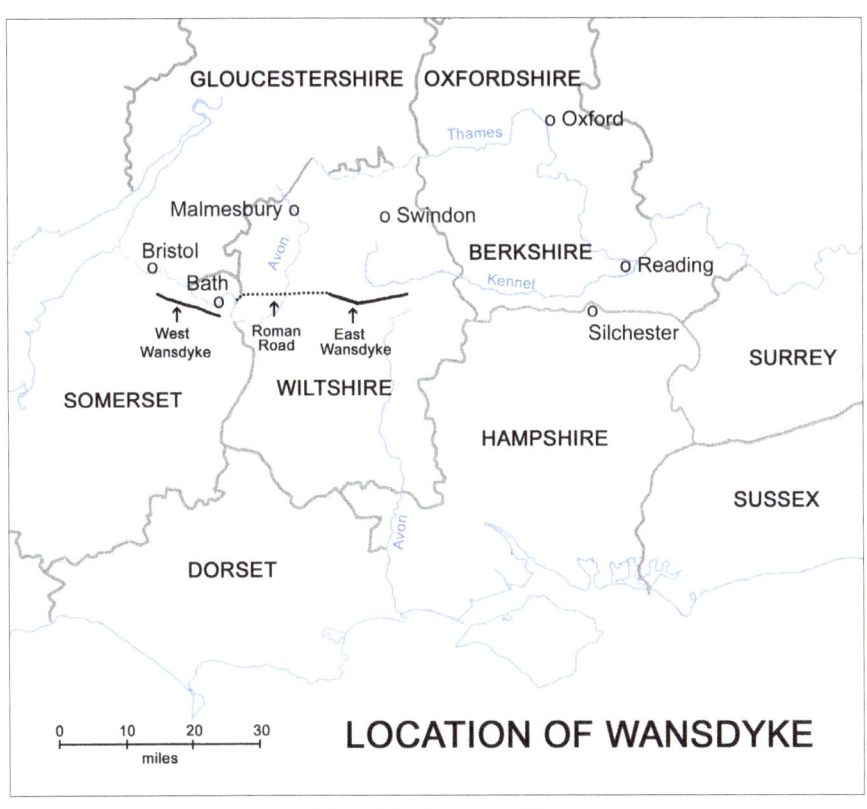

Wansdyke Location Plan

the Devil's Dyke in Cambridgeshire is higher than the highest sections of Wansdyke. This aroused my curiosity. As I tried to read into the subject I found that finding answers to my questions was not straightforward.

There is no single book solely on Wansdyke, which you can simply pick up and find out all the answers. *The Mystery of Wansdyke*, a beautifully illustrated book by Albany Major and Edward Burrow, published in a limited edition in 1926, seemed to be such a book, but is now nearly a hundred years old and, moreover, it took a critical battering from several prominent archaeologists in the 1950s. In 'Wansdyke Reconsidered', Sir Cyril and Lady Aileen Fox, among Major's critics, produced a seminal study based on fieldwork undertaken in the 1950s, which is still important. It is a journal article rather than a book, which was not easy to find when I started this quest, but I am delighted to say it can now be found on the Archaeology Data Service web site. Even this is now sixty years old and much work has been carried out since then which has already led to a number of reappraisals of their work.

That is not to say that there is a paucity of material available. There have been many studies of particular aspects of the dyke. This material falls generally into two categories. The archaeological reports quite rightly spend a lot of time recording their findings, though most also propose a scenario for its construction. I call these the 'bottom-up' sources. Others, the 'top-down' sources, are interested in the wider historical perspective and, when they mention Wansdyke at all, it is as part of a bigger picture and it is therefore not always given a huge amount of attention. It seemed to me that there was a need for a book to fill this gap drawing on both these sources – one that would look at the evidence as rigorously as possible but present it in an accessible manner to encourage the interest in the earthwork which I believe it deserves, while at the same time, bringing all the material together under one cover.

Whilst talking about efforts to raise interest in Wansdyke, it would be remiss of me not to mention Robert Vermaat's excellent website, *Wansdyke 21*, which contains descriptions, maps and photographs of the Dyke and discussion of its origins, which anyone interested in Wansdyke is recommended to explore. However, my work covers aspects which are not discussed on the website, and there has been little activity on it for some years.

What soon becomes apparent is that Wansdyke does not give up its secrets easily. The archaeological finds from the bank itself are relatively few. While they are crucial to understanding its origins they only take us part of the way. In order to go further I have found it necessary to review the history and archaeology of Somerset and Wiltshire throughout the period when the earthwork could have been constructed. This is a long time horizon which spans the end of the Roman occupation of Britain through the coming of the West Saxons, and their territorial disputes with Mercia, to the first incursions of the Vikings. It is a fascinating period, not known as the Dark Ages for nothing. Over the last thirty years or so it has been the subject of much reappraisal, particularly concerning what happened between the departure of the Romans and the coming of the Anglo-Saxons.

This was a period of great change. In the first part of the period in particular the historical sources are few and mostly of doubtful reliability.

The review therefore has to make use of archaeology from the wider area and attempts to fuse this with the historical sources to produce a convincing narrative. As later periods are reached, more reliability can be attached to the historical sources, and a more soundly based narrative can be constructed, though even this is by no means complete and the archaeology remains important. This is a fascinating period for the West Country, a time when many of the features of our modern society were created, and the construction of Wansdyke may even shed some light on what was happening.

I will first describe the earthwork and examine the controversies that have surrounded where each section actually starts and finishes. Wansdyke has fascinated antiquarians and archaeologists since the sixteenth century. I tell the story of these investigations, which leads us to the state of knowledge we now have, and I examine the blind alleys that have been followed along the way. From this we can glean as much as the archaeology will tell us. This is a lot, but not enough on its own. We must turn to the wider historical and archaeological context to try to fill the gaps. Even this will leave us with more than one scenario for the construction of the dyke. Along the way, we will delve into many aspects of early medieval archaeology and history. It has been difficult to construct this as a sequential narrative. For instance, it will be apparent that I do not introduce you to the cast of characters who have constructed this story by their investigations until Chapter 3, and I do not deal with the history of the wider area until Chapter 5. I hope those that are perhaps less familiar with this material will bear with me on this.

One of the many antiquarians to have fallen under the spell of Wansdyke was the renowned Wiltshire archaeologist, Sir Richard Colt Hoare. Writing in 1819, he described his investigations as a chase.

> Many an arduous journey, [he said] has been undertaken, and many successive days have been spent in the deliberate investigation of its course: the chase has been pursued with ardour, and with some degree of success, though, according to the sportsman's natural wish, it has not terminated in death (Colt Hoare 1819 p20).

Unlike Colt Hoare's chase, my work has not been undertaken on horseback in search of something that nobody then quite knew the extent of, nor has it involved further fieldwork, since plenty of fieldwork already exists. This has been a quest undertaken in libraries studying and pulling together the extensive literature that is relevant to Wansdyke. Its aim is to answer the 'who', 'when' and 'why' of Wansdyke. Readers may disagree with my findings but I least they will be able to see how I arrived at them. It is a quest I have found fascinating. What is certain, however, is that I will not be the last person to undertake it. My other aim is to increase awareness of and interest in Wansdyke, which I hope this book will achieve.

Like Colt Hoare's chase, I am delighted to say that my quest has not ended in death either – I am still here to tell the tale!

2

Where is Wansdyke?

Wansdyke is a linear bank and ditch construction that runs in two sections across north Somerset and the Marlborough Downs in Wiltshire in an east-west direction. It is one of the great linear features of England, and yet it seems relatively little known. It is far less famous than, say, Hadrian's Wall or Offa's Dyke, but, after these two great monuments, it is one of the longest and highest linear earthworks we have. The total length from Maes Knoll to New Buildings near Savernake Forest is 35 miles, though 14 miles of this is the 'missing' middle section. Sir Cyril and Lady Aileen Fox described sections of the dyke on the Marlborough Downs in the following terms: 'This is a formidable barrier; the scale exceeds that of the far longer Mercian Dykes, Wat's Dyke and Offa's Dyke on the Welsh border, and of the shorter Bokerly Dyke on the Dorset-Wilts. boundary; only the Devil's Dyke in East Anglia is larger.' (Fox and Fox 1960 p20).

It can be seen from this comment that it fits into a tradition of linear earthworks, of which there are many in Britain. There are several features known as Grimsdyke or Grim's Ditch in different parts of southern England. They are thought to be of Iron Age origin dating to around 300BC and named after 'Grim', another Anglo-Saxon name for Odin. The Romans famously built Hadrian's Wall in the north of England and the Antonine Wall across the narrowest stretch of Central Scotland. Bokerly Dyke is a three mile long ditch on the Dorset-Hampshire border where it meets Wiltshire, possibly built at a similar time to Wansdyke. This will feature again in the story of Wansdyke. On the English-Welsh border are Wat's Dyke and the famous Offa's Dyke. Between Newmarket and Cambridge there are a succession of dykes, the most significant being Devil's Dyke, which seem to be protecting East Anglia from attack from the south-west. There are many more.

The names of these dykes largely come down from Anglo-Saxon charters, and it is relevant to pause at this point to discuss the charters that are relevant to Wansdyke. These provide some of the most important written evidence for the name of the dyke and various features along its length. The Foxes examined the charter evidence in their study, mainly by reference to George Grundy's work on Wiltshire and Somerset charters published in the *Archaeological Journal* (Grundy 1919 and 1920). Charters relating to Stanton St Bernard, Overton and North Newnton in Wiltshire and Bath, South Stoke, Stanton Prior and Marksbury in Somerset mention Wansdyke, usually referring to it as *Woden's dic* or similar, and to features on it. These charters mostly date from the 9th or 10th centuries, and are concerned with defining plots of land which are to be transferred from one owner to another. Other charters are relevant to the discussion of possible extensions to the dyke.

In describing the dyke, I will refer to the section running across north Somerset as West Wansdyke and the section running across Wiltshire as East Wansdyke. I will start with the eastern section which is the better preserved and most spectacular today. In the case of both sections, there is controversy about where they start and end, a north-west extension to West Wansdyke and an eastern extension to East Wansdyke being postulated. I will then examine the 'missing' middle section. In this chapter I will concentrate on the topography of Wansdyke rather than its form and structure, which will be addressed in the fourth chapter.

I have, of course, walked much of the area myself, but I have also drawn heavily on the detailed description of the dyke by Sir Cyril and Lady Aileen Fox (Fox and Fox 1960), updating this with newer information where relevant. I have also drawn upon the information in the *Wansdyke21* website, which contains descriptions and many maps and photographs of the earthwork as well as many of Edward Burrow's drawings from *The Mystery of Wansdyke* (Vermaat 1999a).

East Wansdyke

East Wansdyke runs in almost continuous form from Morgan's Hill between Calne and Devizes to New Buildings about half a mile west of Savernake Forest. It runs mostly across the high ground of the Marlborough Downs with good visibility to the north in many places. As previously mentioned, the location of the ditch on the north side of the earthwork indicates that it was built by those living on its southern side

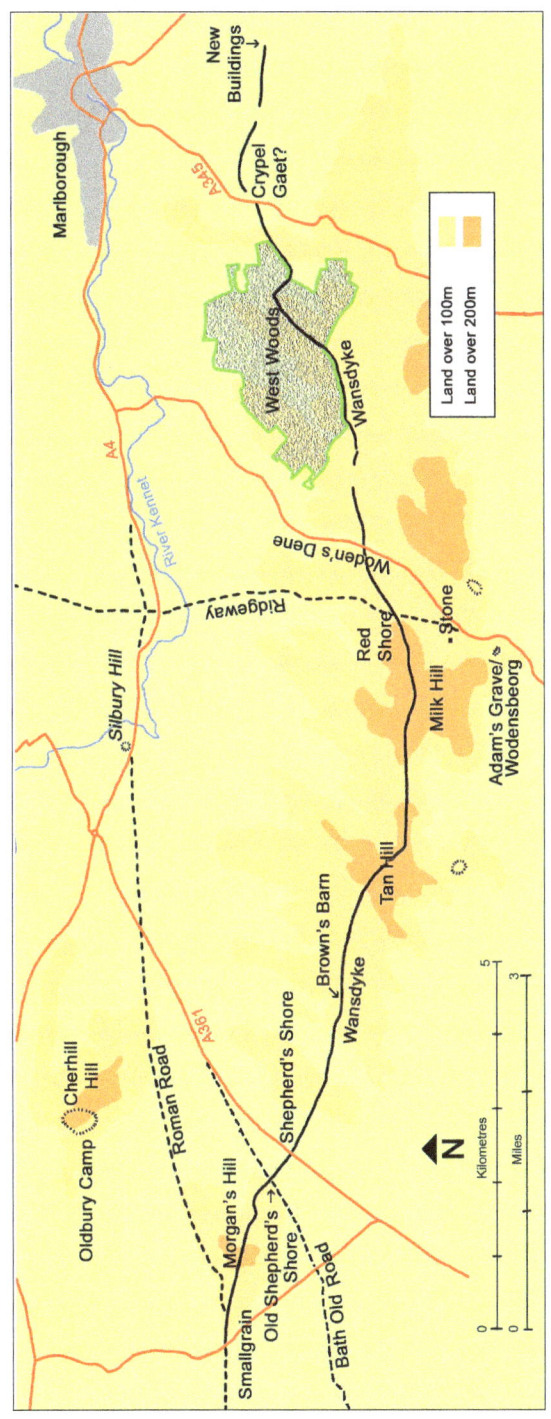

East Wansdyke. Contains OS data © Crown copyright Open Data 2008.

Track on line of Roman Road meets Wansdyke at Morgan's Hill

as it was the combination of bank and ditch which presented the more formidable obstacle.

Fox and Fox comment that the terminus of the ditch at Morgan's Hill practically coincides with the change from the Middle to the Lower chalk, which is a richer soil, and with the end of the plateau. Woodland may well have been prevalent to the west which might have formed a protective flank to the ditch (Fox and Fox 1960 p6). I will discuss this later in relation to the missing middle section.

At its western end the earthwork is intersected by the Bath to London Roman Road. This was one of the major highways of Roman times which also connected to the Roman towns of *Cunetio* (near Mildenhall east of Marlborough) and *Calleva Atrebatum* (Silchester) to the east. The connection to the Roman road at this point originally led scholars to conclude that the *agger* or bank on which the road was built was in fact the course of Wansdyke to the west of Morgan's Hill. However, Fox and Fox indicate that the road was effectively put out of action at the western end of the ditch:

> the inference is clear; the builders of Wansdyke have entirely disregarded
> the road as a potential boundary, digging half of it away when they made

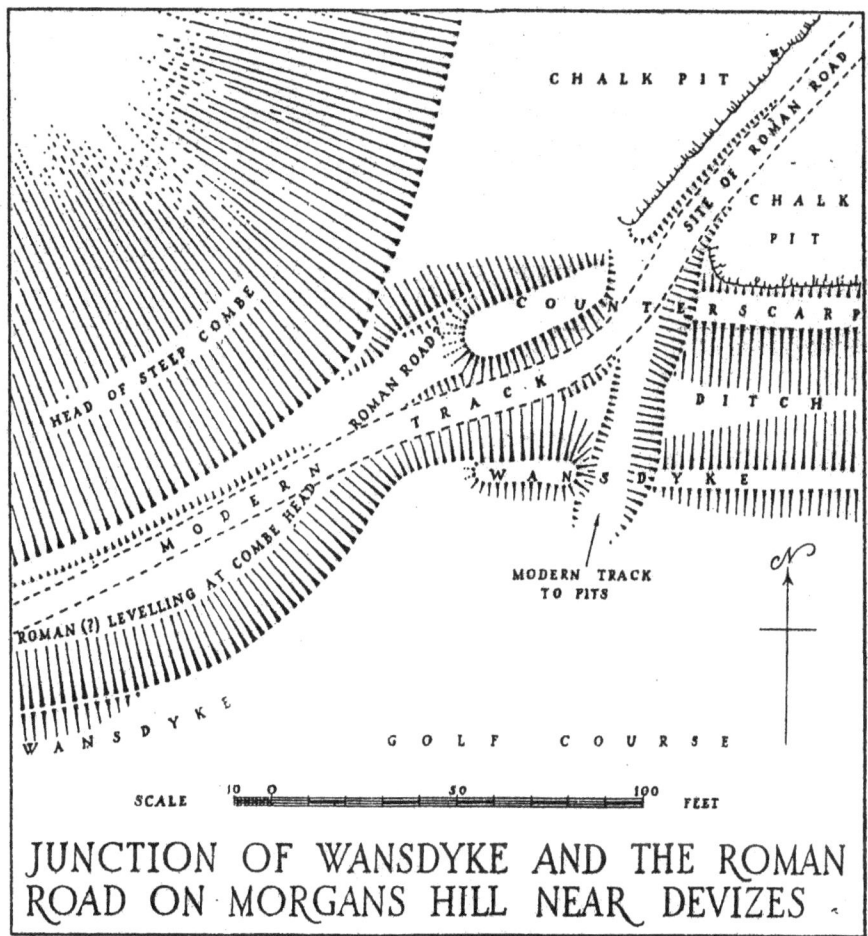

JUNCTION OF WANSDYKE AND THE ROMAN ROAD ON MORGANS HILL NEAR DEVIZES

Fox's Map of Junction between Wansdyke and Roman Road (Archaeological Journal 1958, Royal Archaeological Institute. York, Archaeology Data Service (distributor) (doi : 10.5284/1068668)

their ditch, and incorporating the remainder in their counterscarp bank, which retains the characteristic angular Roman embankment scarp on the outer side (Fox and Fox 1960 pp5-6).

Approaching Wansdyke from the north east along the track which follows the course of the Roman road, it makes a sharp turn to the right to align with what became Wansdyke (see photo above). The Foxes argued that the level of the road was much lower than the track in Roman times. Wansdyke came shooting down Morgan's Hill from

Wansdyke at Morgan's Hill

the left with its counterscarp (the lower, outer bank on the north side of the ditch) completely obliterating the road. Initially, they believed, Wansdyke terminated here on the edge of the steep combe which falls away to the right, the remaining 300 metres being added later. These 300 metres followed the course of the Roman road which was now in the ditch of the earthwork. Thus the Roman road was completely blocked. This becomes important dating evidence indicating that the dyke was built later than the construction of the Roman road.

Looking east, the line of the dyke and the Roman road diverge here, the road descending in a north easterly direction towards Silbury Hill while the dyke continues its more south-easterly course along the ridge to Morgan's Hill. Morgan's Hill is a prime vantage point to the north, looking out towards Oldbury Castle, the Iron Age hillfort above the Cherhill White Horse. However, the ditch follows the southern slope of the hill, not the northern slope as might be expected. The Foxes suggest that this was to shorten the distance of the constructed earthwork (Fox and Fox 1960 p10), and given the extent of the diversion that would be necessary to follow the northern side of the hill this may be true.

The dyke is particularly pronounced here. Between Morgan's Hill and Old Shepherd's Shore is the location of the first of Augustus Pitt Rivers' hugely important excavations, that of 1889, at which Romano-British coarse pottery, an iron knife and nails were found on the old ground surface and coarse pottery in the body of the rampart (Pitt Rivers 1892 p26).

East of Morgan's Hill the earthwork drops away gently to Old Shepherd's Shore, where it crosses the old Bath to London road, now an unmetalled byway. Here there is a substantial break in the ditch at which are located two tumuli, and this may well be an original gate in the dyke. Beyond this, in the bottom of a dry valley the dyke crosses the A361 Devizes to Swindon road at what is now simply called Shepherd's Shore.

View towards Avebury from Wansdyke showing Silbury Hill

Beyond Shepherd's Shore, the dyke climbs back up to the high ground of Bishop's Canning Down, again for a time taking the southern slope. Here begins the longest uninterrupted stretch of the dyke extending about 5½ miles to the Alton Barnes-Lockeridge Road at Wodensdene. Just over a mile east of Shepherd's Shore, at a location called Brown's Barn by Pitt Rivers, are the remains of a Romano-British enclosure, one side of which has been obliterated by the dyke. It was here that Pitt Rivers dug further trenches in 1890 and 1891, finding an iron cleat and more pottery, and demonstrating that the dyke had been built over the enclosure (Pitt Rivers 1892 pp26-28). These finds proved Wansdyke was constructed during or after the Roman period.

This stretch of the dyke over Tan Hill and Milk Hill has superb views to the north across the Kennet Valley, and is the location referred to in my introduction. In this area a number of older cross ditches are built over by the dyke. On Milk Hill, where the parish boundary between Stanton St Bernard and Alton Barnes crosses Wansdyke, is the location of the earliest charter record we encounter to mention the dyke by name. Here it is referred to as *Wodnes Dic* in three charters recording royal grants of land in Stanton St Bernard to Ordlaf (903) (Sawyer S368, Grundy 1919 p 210 nb Grundy gives the date as 905) and the Bishop of Ramsbury (957 and 960). They also mention an earthwork, *Eald Burh,* and a pond, *Oxna Mere,* which lie on the boundary. The former can be seen on the modern OS map. The charter to Ordlaf is the one that first mentions *Wodnes Dic.* An earlier charter of 825 for nearby Alton Priors refers to 'thaere *Ealden Dic'* - the Old Ditch, which is thought to be the earliest reference to Wansdyke in a charter (Fox and Fox 1960 pp12-14, S272).

East of Milk Hill is Red Shore, where Wansdyke crosses the Ridgeway, the ancient north-south trackway predating the earthwork. This is referred to as *thaet Riad Geat* in the Alton Priors Charter (Fox and Fox 1960 p14). Again, a substantial break in the ditch can be observed which is thought to be an original gate, and there is possibly a trace of an outer earthwork extending north from the western bank which could have been part of the gate. The gate and the adjoining stretches of dyke are now well wooded and only passable with difficulty in places. It should be noted that from Milk Hill the dyke turns slightly north east, sufficiently so to take it off the highest ground for the rest of its course.

From Red Shore the ditch descends to the Alton Barnes-Lockeridge Road at Woden's Dene. This is thought to be the location known as *Woddes Gaet,* which is the subject of some controversy. *Woddes Gaet* is mentioned in the Alton Priors Charter. Reference is made to a great

Woddes Geat Stone, photographed by Robert Vermaat

stone, acting as a boundary marker, lying in the middle of the bottom of
the Dene that runs to *Woddes Gaet:*

*Thonon on otherne Micelne Stan on tham Wege middan on thaere Daene
Bytnan the ligeth ut on Woddes Gaet .*

Then to the other Great Stone to the Track in the middle of the bottom
of the Dean which runs to Woden's Gate (Grundy 1919 p 162, Fox and
Fox 1960 p14).

Fox and Fox suggest that there was a gate created here in late
Saxon times, though they note that George Grundy took the view that
it may have been further south on the track to *Wodnesbeorge* (ibid p14).
Peter Fowler takes the view that this is an original gate made when the
ditch was first constructed (Fowler 2001 p189). Vermaat, on the other
hand, suggests that the boulder shown on the plan on page 98 of *The
Mystery of Wansdyke* lying near Red Shore might be the one referred to
in the charter, and that Red Shore and Woddes Gaet are one and the

Knap Hill   Vale of Pewsey   Adam's Grave

View from Ridgeway looking south

same (Vermaat 1999a). I am not convinced that the stone photographed by Vermaat (pictured overleaf) is the same one as illustrated by Burrow as it is in a different location and of different dimensions, though its present position, surrounded by other stones, does not look original. The charter bounds refer to the *Daene Bytnan* (the valley bottom) which describes the line of the modern road rather than Red Shore, which is quite elevated. I am therefore persuaded by Fowler's position.

The Foxes speculated that there was something special about this particular area given multiple references to Woden in *Woddes Dene*, *Woddes Gaet* and *Wodensbeorg*, the latter being the neolithic long barrow now known as Adam's Grave a mile and a half south of the dyke. Certainly the view to the south across the Vale of Pewsey to Salisbury Plain, flanked by Knap Hill and Adam's Grave, is spectacular.

The next stretch of Wansdyke has been studied in detail by Peter Fowler. His extremely interesting findings are set out in 'Wansdyke In The Woods' in *Roman Wiltshire and After: Papers in Honour of Ken Annable* (Fowler 2001). This stretch of Wansdyke is particularly unusual because it passes through woodland. Previous work done by Fowler (Fowler

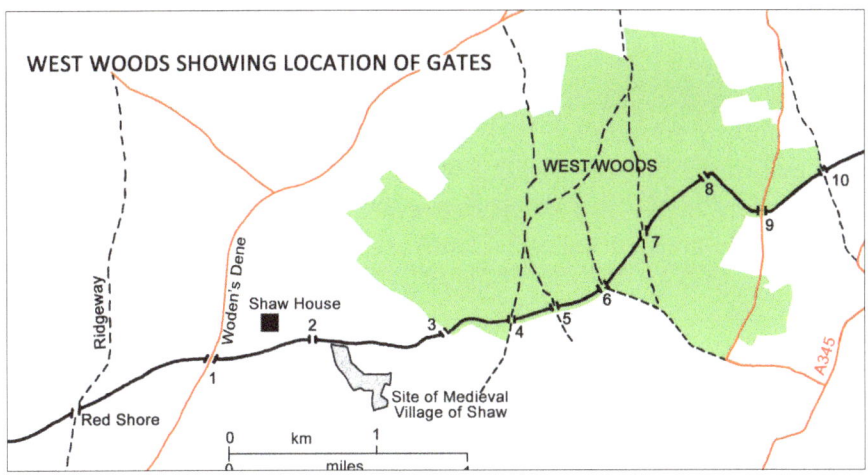

1. Woddes Geat – referred to in spurious charter S272;
2. Old Shaw – existence unproven;
3. 'Triangle Gate' – an invented name;
4. Eadgardes Gete – referred to in charter S784
5. 'Meux Gate' – invented name for a nameless break;
6. Titferth's Gate – referred to in charter S449;
7. 'Readdan Gate' – invented name for nameless break;
8. 'Broadleat Gate' – invented name for original 70m break in earthwork;
9. 'Clatford Park Gate' – invented name for possible undocumented gate at junction with track along Clatford bottom;
10. 'Short Oak Gate' – invented name for modern break, but could be location of Cripel Gate referred to in charter S424.

(Fowler 2001 pp188-191)

West Woods showing Fowler's Gates. Contains OS data © Crown copyright Open Data 2008.

2000) demonstrates that the wood was extant at the time the earthwork was created. This is surprising, because of all the likely functions of Wansdyke the need to see and be seen seems all-important and this is not possible in the woods. The earthwork here is much diminished in scale compared to the stretches across the Marlborough Downs, with the Foxes identifying a sudden diminution in scale over the course of 300 yards on the site of Old Shaw House, which corresponds with a change from upper chalk to chalk with flints (Fox and Fox 1960 p23).

Many of Fowler's conclusions belong in later chapters, but here I will describe his conclusions on the overall layout of the dyke. He identifies up to ten possible 'gates' in the stretch of Wansdyke between *Woddes Gaet* and Short Oak Copse. These gates meet north-south trackways, which Fowler proposes are a bundle of tracks forming a north-south transhumant 'Ridgeway Route' newly developing in Roman times from the ancient Ridgeway (Fowler 2001 pp193-195). This route was too important to simply block and ways through it needed to be constructed which were able to control the traffic using the route and repel enemies if necessary. Nowadays, the sole trackway known as the Ridgeway meets Wansdyke at Red Shore, which should probably be considered with Fowler's gates, though it was not part of his study.

With the exception of a proposed gate at Old Shaw, all the gates appear today as essentially no more than breaks in the ditch. It is suggested by Fowler that they could have had some sort of stockade arrangement to accompany them, which would have made them look very much like gates. Fieldwork shows that some are very likely to be part of the original construction, while evidence for others may have been destroyed by the creation of newer openings. Three of them are mentioned in charters: *Woddes Gaet* (see above), *Edgardes Gete* (West Overton Charter 972) and *Titferth's Geat* (East Overton Charter 939), while a fourth, the gate at Short Oak Copse at the eastern end of the series of gates, could be *Cripel Gaet,* referred to in the Oare Charter, though a location on the A345 is also possible (Fowler 2001 p188).

Fowler argues that there are clear parallels with Hadrian's Wall, which could well have been well known to the builders of Wansdyke. Although Hadrian's Wall was built of stone, the other great 'wall' across Scotland, the Antonine Wall is a precedent for a bank and ditch construction. In other respects, Hadrian's Wall was intended to 'separate the Romans from the Barbarians' but more recent work suggests it was also to control movement (Fowler 2001 p195). Most interestingly, Fowler draws a parallel between the gates and the milecastles on Hadrian's Wall. He proposes a series of gates at roughly 800 yard intervals, provision far more lavish than required, as on Hadrian's Wall, which gave easy access to people wishing to pass through but they could also allow troops to move easily through the wall to deal with an attack from the north (Fowler 2001 p194). He argues that the whole design of this stretch of Wansdyke was intended to funnel all travellers, and potential invaders, off the chalk and into this section of the wall, where control of access could be concentrated.

Wansdyke continues for about 1.5 miles beyond the A345, in much reduced form, terminating quite suddenly at New Buildings in open countryside about three quarters of a mile west of Savernake Forest. This section is difficult to access from public rights of way, with footpaths crossing it at two locations only. This was identified with some certainty by the Foxes as the eastern end of the earthwork, but there has long been debate about possible further eastward extensions.

The Eastward Extension of Wansdyke

The Rev John Collinson was probably the first to postulate a line for Wansdyke extending beyond New Buildings. He had it commencing at Andover in his *History and Antiquities of the County of Somerset* of 1792 (*op cit* Vol I p.xxiii). Sir Richard Colt Hoare accused him of committing a 'great error', since, in his view, the earthworks referred to were not part of Wansdyke (Colt Hoare 1819 p20). Colt Hoare had his own ideas on an the eastward extension of Wansdyke. He identified Bedwyn Dyke and fragments of ditch in Shalbourne and Inkpen Parishes as parts of Wansdyke and believed it might extend as far as Silchester, the capital of the *civitas* of the Atrebates in Roman times, though he conceded that he had no evidence for this (ibid p33). This view has been endorsed by others (Major and Burrow 1926; Collingwood and Myers 1956; Crawford 1954), indeed Major and Burrow revived Collinson's idea of a southern branch leading to Ludgershall. Wansdyke is shown on old Ordnance Survey Maps extending beyond Savernake Forest and it is often stated that Inkpen, in Berkshire, is the eastern terminus.

Two articles looked at this in some detail; O G S Crawford's 1953 article 'The East End of Wansdyke', published in the *Wiltshire Archaeological and Natural History Magazine* in 1954, and the Foxes' work.

Crawford's starting point was that an excavation carried out in 1924 by Mr H C Brentnall of Marlborough College, east of New Buildings, had proved that the dyke continued beyond this point (Crawford 1954 p119). Albany Major, who was involved with these investigations, claims that they had located the course of the dyke across a field south of New Buildings and across the railway line that then existed, entering

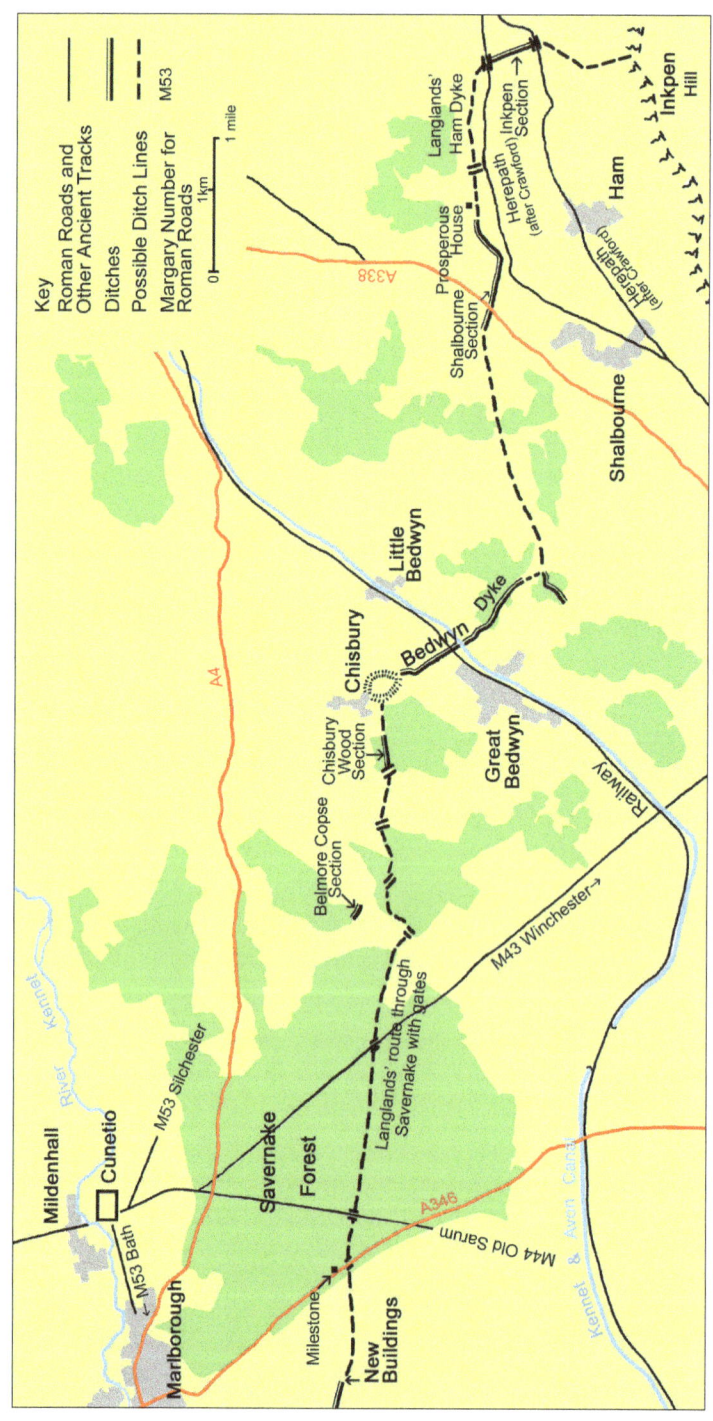

Suggested Eastern Extension to East Wansdyke. Contains OS data © Crown copyright Open Data 2008/2015.

Savernake Forest close to the second milestone from Marlborough on the Marlborough-Andover Road (A346) (Major and Burrow 1926 p104).

In fact, two excavations were carried out during the summer of 1924, the first twenty feet inside the boundary of Savernake Forest in the vicinity of Great Lodge Bottom, directed by Brentnall and Major together, and the second eighteen feet east of the visible termination of the dyke at New Buildings, directed by Brentnall alone. The first dig uncovered a bank with a ditch on each side, albeit that the southern ditch was described as very shallow. However, its very existence should have aroused suspicions that this was not Wansdyke. No dateable relics were found. They tried in vain to establish a connection to a bank which Major had previously traced running a long way into the Forest on the south side of Great Lodge Bottom. They were forced to accept that the banks could be connected with the building of the 'Great Lodge' which tradition places in this location, but they did not 'relinquish the idea that the line of a pre-existing dyke was reconstituted for the purpose' (Brentnall 1924 p72).

Accepting that this evidence was inconclusive, they decided to attack the problem from the New Buildings end. Brentnall had dug a trench there the previous year based on aerial photographs provided to him by Crawford. This showed the existence of an ancient hedge bank system into which the ditch, described as a drought line ditch, undoubtedly fell. Major was unavailable for this second dig, so Brentnall determined to dig his trench 18 feet (5.5m) beyond the last vestige of the dyke at New Buildings starting on the projected axis of the dyke and extending northwards from it at right angles. At 15 feet (4.6m) north of the axis line to the dyke the start of a downward slope was discernible. However, the further he dug the deeper the silted material became. At 25' 6' (7.8m) north of the axis line a hearth was found. Despite digging a total of 32 feet (9.8m) north of the axis no northern side of the ditch was discovered. At that point cost dictated that the digging had to stop (*ibid* pp72/74).

Brentnall noticed that measurements taken on the existing dyke before its termination had shown it narrowing in a manner which suggested to him that about 15-20 feet of its width in this final section had been removed at the same time as the bank had been totally destroyed beyond it. Consequently, the axis of the bank could be several feet further north than they had estimated and he felt confident that the outer edge of the ditch would have been encountered if they had dug a further 5 or 6 feet. On the basis of this he was able to conclude that '. . . it seems clear enough that Wansdyke did not always end where it ends today.' (ibid p74),

This seems much less convincing to me than it did to Brentnall. He did not publish any sections to help us understand his findings better and he did not produce any dating evidence. The hearth that he found is unlikely to have been connected to Wansdyke as it is not the sort of use that would be expected to be found hard up against a major territorial boundary. While its subsequent construction could have obliterated the ditch it is equally the case that there may have been no ditch in the first place and that everything he thought was a ditch was in fact connected to the hearth. An equally plausible explanation for the narrowing of the bank was that the builders of Wansdyke were coming to the limit of their territory and were running out of material from the ditch to build the bank. I think that 'not proven' is the best that could be said about this evidence.

No-one other than Crawford seems to have relied on the evidence of these excavations subsequently. It may be noted that he had also assisted with this project by providing aerial photographs, so maybe he felt he had some sort of stake in it. However, the purpose of his investigations seemed to be to determine the line of the dyke east of New Buildings rather than any concerns about the principle of whether it extended beyond New Buildings in the first place. The Foxes took a more sceptical view (Fox and Fox 1960 pp 18-20).

There are five sections of ditch which are potential candidates for extensions of Wansdyke, all originally identified by Colt Hoare. Starting from the west, there is a short section of bank about 200 yards long on the eastern fringe of Savernake Forest on the southern edge of Belmore Copse, which faces north east. The Foxes believed this to be the product of levelling up after quarrying in the area and noted that Crawford had also concluded that this was unlikely to be part of Wansdyke. About a mile to the east of this is a stretch of ditch running across the north of Chisbury Wood. This shows no sign of emerging from the woods and is described by the Foxes as 'negligible in scale, character and extent'. They note that Crawford also considered this doubtful.

The most imposing of these candidate sections is Bedwyn Dyke. This is a bank and ditch of comparable size to Wansdyke at its reduced scale in West Woods, which extends for over a mile running south from Chisbury hill fort. It faces east, on which basis it was thought to provide some sort of enclosure for the lands to the south west. The dyke ends at Round Copse, having begun to turn westwards at its southern end. The Foxes considered that there was no valid reason for calling this part of Wansdyke. They noted that the dyke was nameless in both the Little Bedwyn Charter of 778 and the Great Bedwyn Charter of 968. In their opinion, the westward curve at the southern end of the dyke made it likely to be a local defence work and in essence a cross valley dyke (see plan above) (Fox and Fox 1960 p19).

American archaeologists Hostetter and Howe made a more detailed examination of Bedwyn Dyke in the 1980s as part of a study of the Romano-British villa at Castle Copse, Great Bedwyn. They identified it as different in character to Wansdyke both in scale and in the way the sections of dyke lie on the land. The earthworks usually appear to consist of a single bank and ditch with a total width of 15 metres generally facing north and east and appearing to close gaps in open terrain between forested areas. Unlike Wansdyke, it contains sections which 'jog' at right angles. They concluded, like the Foxes, that it was a system of cross-valley dykes and not part of Wansdyke (Hostetter and Howe 1997 p359).

The Shalbourne section is a 700 yard section of earthwork, running from the Shalbourne stream just below East Court towards Prosperous Farm, where it peters out. This shows up well on aerial photographs taken by Major George Allen before the Second World War. Crawford notes that Prosperous Farm was the home of Jethro Tull from 1709 to 1741, and it might be no surprise if this champion of horse-hoeing had little regard for an ancient earthwork. Crawford also noted that this section of dyke blocked the Salisbury to Wantage road (Crawford 1954 pp 122-4). The Foxes again thought this unlikely to be part of Wansdyke (Fox and Fox 1960 p20).

The final section is a three-quarters of a mile stretch running north-south along Old Dyke Lane in Inkpen Parish in Berkshire to a point just beyond the Wiltshire boundary. The north-south alignment might be considered strange, but less than half a mile further south is the 350 metre escarpment leading up to the chalk downs near Inkpen

Beacon and Walbury Camp, which would be expected to provide a better terminal point. However, Crawford found no trace of a continuation across the intervening ground. This section of dyke blocks an ancient track known as the Pewsey herepath (Crawford 1954 p 124). The Foxes note that the Inkpen Dyke has a name of its own in the Buttermere Charter of the 9th Century, namely *readan dic,* The Red Dyke, and again found this to be evidence that this section of ditch was not part of Wansdyke (Fox and Fox 1960 p20).

If it had been proved that the earthwork extended to the western edge of Savernake Forest this does not necessarily prove the case for a significant further extension. Nonetheless, the Foxes were puzzled that Wansdyke did not penetrate further into Savernake Forest in order to control the two Roman roads that run through it (M43 and M44 according to the numbering system devised by Ivan Margary - see plan above). These are the roads running from Cirencester via *Cunetio* to Old Sarum and Winchester respectively. They concluded either that these roads had fallen out of use by the time the dyke was built or that the dyke 'was constructed far enough into the Forest to cover existing clearings made by Wiltshire folk and that it indicates the tentative limits of settlement at the time Wansdyke was built' (ibid p18).

Robert Vermaat puts forward the proposal that Wansdyke ends at New Buildings because it is a late Roman or post Roman construction designed to address a conflict between two groupings of Britons (Vermaat 1999a Section 10). At this time they would have been occupying the *civitates* of the Roman Empire. The end of Wansdyke probably coincides very closely with the boundary between the *civitates* of the Belgae and the Atrebates. The dyke ends here simply because to go any further would have taken it into Atrebatic territory. Bruce Eagles has suggested that what would become the western boundary of the Kinwardstone Hundred could have formed the boundary between the Belgae and the Atrebates, on the basis of small differences in the archaeology of this area, which seems to have links with neighbouring areas of Berkshire and Hampshire (Atrebatic territory), while the area around Salisbury, seems to have stronger links with the south coast and the Isle of Wight, which belonged to the Belgae (Eagles 2018 p6). New Buildings is very close indeed to the western boundary of the hundred. We will see later that there is evidence that Savernake Forest once extended further west than it does now, so maybe Wansdyke extended to its previous edge.

Hundreds were a medieval unit of local government, thought to take their name from the fact that they originally measured about 100 *hides,* a hide being the amount of land required to support a household. They probably date back to about the tenth century. The Kinwardstone Hundred contains a group of parishes on the eastern edge of Wiltshire, bordering both Berkshire and Hampshire. It was one of the largest hundreds in Wiltshire, and is thought to be based on a *Villa Regalis* at Great Bedwyn (Langlands 2019 p 131). It has been studied in detail by Alexander Langlands, one of the advocates of the argument that Wansdyke was a frontier between Wessex and Mercia and dates from the seventh or eighth centuries. A key part of this argument is that Wansdyke extended well into and beyond Savernake Forest. At the heart of the hundred is the Iron Age hillfort of Chisbury believed to be the location of one of King Alfred's *burhs.*

Langlands has interrogated a number of charters relating to land in the hundred dating from the tenth century, and all but one thought to be reliable. He has traced a line of possible gates occurring at regular intervals along the estate boundaries, which are mentioned in the charters, two of them located on the M43 and M44 Roman roads. He comments that the regularity with which these seven gates feature along a five mile stretch of boundary echo the Roman milecastle theory put forward by Peter Fowler in respect of West Woods. These connect a point close to Savernake Church, less than a mile east of New Buildings, with Chisbury in a fairly straight line. Further gates can be identified at the southern end of the Bedwyn Dykes and adjacent to the isolated stretches of dyke in Shalbourne and Inkpen Parishes (Langlands 2019 pp129-134). This clearly supports the view that Wansdyke does extend beyond New Buildings and, as such, forms part of a much longer boundary.

And finally, tantalisingly, there appears to be a shadow on aerial photos extending in a gentle arc from the east end of Wansdyke to the A346 about a quarter of a mile north of the church (see overleaf)!

West Wansdyke

For the purposes of this section, I am treating West Wansdyke as the section running from Maes Knoll on the edge of Bristol to Odd Down on

This aerial photo shows the 'shadow' extending east from New Buildings
(copyright of Wiltshire and Swindon Historic Environment Record)

the edge of Bath, a distance of 9 miles. Compared with East Wansdyke, West Wansdyke is, today, very much the poor relation. It has been badly eroded by ploughing over the years as it crosses much better arable land than the downs over which East Wansdyke passes. Indeed, the Foxes state: 'The injury done to it of recent years is serious: at our urgent request the best preserved portions were scheduled by the Ministry of Works in 1956' (Fox and Fox 1960 p 26). In many places the bank appears as little more than a 'ripple of earth' running across a field, while in others it could be mistaken for a hedge bank. In very few places does it stand comparison with its eastern counterpart. For the explorer the problem is compounded by the fact that there is very little public access to the western section. Public footpaths invariably run across the line of the dyke, rather than along it, so that only small sections can be observed at a time.

The dyke also crosses much less dramatic terrain than East Wansdyke. This is complex landscape with fewer grand vistas, described as 'undulating and structurally confused' by the Foxes (ibid p28). Moreover, the dyke is by no means continuous. In some places this is due to ploughing out and in others it seems it was never there in the

Publow Hill   Stantonbury

View from Maes Knoll looking east along the line of West Wansdyke

first place. The Foxes, therefore, relied to some extent on the findings of Sir Richard Colt Hoare, recorded in the early 19th century when well over 100 years less plough damage had occurred. We can also now refer to the first systematic archaeological investigation of West Wansdyke, undertaken as joint venture between the Avon Archaeological Unit and English Heritage in 1996. This work was recorded in an article for the *Archaeological Journal* by Jonathan Erskine entitled 'The West Wansdyke: An Appraisal of the Dating, Dimensions and Construction Techniques in the Light of The Excavated Evidence' (2007). These are the excavations referred to in this section.

Stantonbury, the hillfort in the middle of this section, was a point from which the whole length of West Wansdyke from Maes Knoll to Odd Down could be seen. It may well have been the point from which the line of the dyke was originally planned (Fox and Fox 1960 p32). Sadly, its value as a viewpoint has been diminished by the woodland which now covers its slopes, and which obscures most views from the fort. Maes Knoll, by contrast, remains open and good views can be had to Stantonbury and the horizon beyond on the line of the Fosse Way. In the photograph above, the line of the dyke can be followed dipping

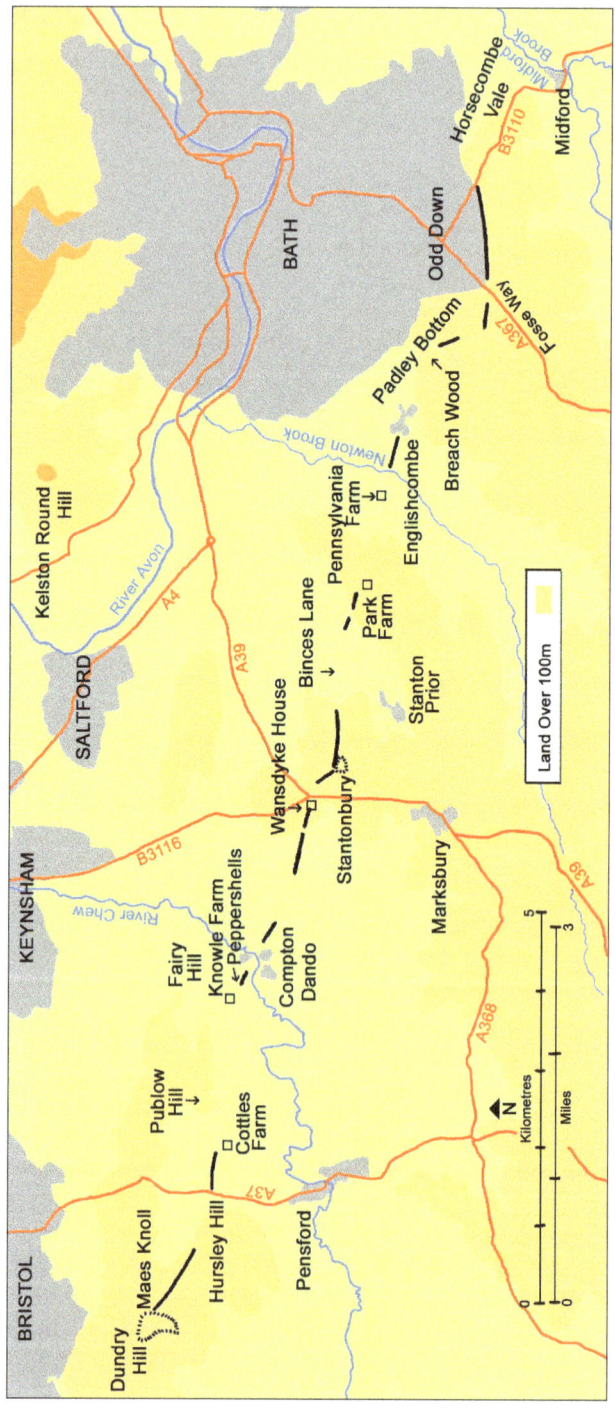

West Wansdyke. Contains OS data © Crown copyright Open Data 2011.

down into the Chew Valley and rising up again to Stantonbury. What is also evident is the way the land rises to the left of the view, which is to the north of the dyke. Publow Hill can be seen in the middle distance with Stantonbury Hill beyond it. Publow Hill, together with Fairy Hill, forms a minor ridge line on which, for the most part, the dyke is on the southern side, thus having its view across the Avon Valley obscured.

In this section the dyke leaves the rampart of Maes Knoll in a smooth curve, like the junction of a branch line leaving the main railway line, to plunge down the side of the hill in a wooded corridor to a minor road at Norton Malreward. A mile beyond the road, it crosses Hursley Hill, now the A37 but probably a route of importance in antiquity. The crossing is, however, obliterated by the construction of the North Somerset Railway in 1873 (Erskine 2007 p100) and the modern A37 which is three lanes wide at this point. Colt Hoare described the bank and ditch as very visible on both sides of the road in his day. There is a good section of dyke between the A37 and Cottles Farm but both Colt Hoare and the Foxes recorded no trace of it east of Publow Brook and over Publow Hill. The Foxes noted that neither air photography nor fieldwork had succeeded in finding any real trace of the dyke here (Fox and Fox 1960 p37 and see Colt Hoare 1819 p23). Crawford had also noted this gap, and speculated that the River Chew and the brook acted as the boundary (Crawford 1953 p253). This seems unlikely. The brook is a very minor barrier in defensive terms. Also, elsewhere it duplicates areas where the dyke is present, running north of the A37 to Cottles Farm section, before turning south to run into the River Chew, which is half a mile south of the dyke at this point.

The archaeological excavations of 1996 in the area around Slate Lane and Fairy Hill yielded 'no significant evidence', though a note by the author suggests some evidence at Fairy Hill (Erskine 2007 pp 84 and 94). However, these sites seem a bit off-line compared to the section of the dyke that re-emerges east of Peppershells Wood on the edge of Compton Dando, and may be compared to the sites Major identified south of Wooscombe Bottom which Crawford roundly condemned as 'wrong' (Crawford 1953b p253). Colt Hoare noticed the dyke at Knowle Farm west of Peppershells (Colt Hoare 1819 p23).

The River Chew is crossed at Compton Dando. While rising up a valley east of the river, the dyke is in a reasonable state of preservation,

but again it has its view northwards obscured by the high ground of Lye
Hill. It attains higher ground west of Wansdyke House, which is at the
junction of the A39 and the B3116, before climbing the north west side
of Stantonbury Hill. This is now one of the most impressive sections of
West Wansdyke.

Stantonbury is descended on its east side, and the dyke disappears
east of the road from Stanton Prior. Colt Hoare described the dyke as
'visible' across the first field east of the road, which he called Wansdyke
Piece. Thereafter, it became less visible across a ploughed field, a lane

Wansdyke on Stantonbury Hill

(Binces Lane) and two further fields before re-emerging in a 'very
decided and perfect manner' on the east side of the Corston Brook (Colt
Hoare 1819 p24). This was the site of further archaeological excavations
in 1996 which found evidence of the dyke in trenches either side of
Binces Lane (Erskine 2007 pp 85-87).

Having descended to Corston Brook at Dog Kennel Wood, the line
of the dyke climbs steeply up to Park Farm, known as Newton Farm in

Colt Hoare's day. Here, the Foxes noted that the dyke was crossed by an ancient ridgeway, one of the branches of the Jurassic Way mentioned in the Bath Abbey Charter of 963 as a herepath (Fox and Fox 1960 p 32). From here there are extensive views across the valley of the Newton Brook to Odd Down and the line of the Fosse Way.

From Park Farm the line of the dyke descends to the Brook just below Pennsylvania Farm. Colt Hoare could not find it in this section but the Foxes traced it from an aerial photo (Colt Hoare 1891 p25, Fox and Fox 1960 p 32). Evidence of the dyke was found in an excavation east of Park Farm (Erskine 2007). The Foxes identified another gap in the construction east of Pennsylvania Farm, extending about ¼ mile, though they were less certain about this than other gaps. Certainly, the dyke reappears east of Pennsylvania Farm as it crosses the Newton Brook and climbs up toward Englishcombe Village. Here, not unexpectedly, it disappears again, having been obliterated by the development of the village.

East of Englishcombe, the line of the dyke turns south, running along the west side of the Padley Bottom. The Foxes identified this as another gap in the construction, noting that 'Padley Bottom would have provided a formidable barrier under primitive conditions when its slopes were densely wooded and this may explain the absence of the dyke here' (Fox and Fox 1960 p 35). Wansdyke re-emerges to the south of Breach Wood, climbing up towards Middle Wood before turning east again to run along the contours through Vernham Wood to the A367 Bath-Radstock Road, which is the line of the Fosse Way. The Fosse Way was, of course, a major strategic route in Roman times, and the builders of Wansdyke would undoubtedly have wished to control it. It may therefore be expected that there would have been a gate at this point, of the type which has already been noted on East Wansdyke. However, the construction of the modern A367 has obliterated any trace that may have existed of such a gate.

East of the A367, Wansdyke follows a straight course along the backs of houses to the B3110 Midford Road opposite the Cross Keys Pub. Unfortunately, the gardens of these houses have obliterated much of the ditch and forward slope of the dyke. At the B3110 is a sign, erected to commemorate the now defunct Wansdyke Council, named after the dyke. However, this is not quite the end of the dyke. The Foxes identified the springhead at the top of Horsecombe Vale about 300 yards north of the B3110, even in their time obliterated by houses, as the end of West Wansdyke. They comment: 'There is no evidence that the dyke went further. The Bath charter makes no mention of a *dic* other than at Horsecombe. Horsecombe Vale would have been a formidable barrier to north-south movement' (ibid p36).

Both Colt Hoare and Major and Burrow were convinced that the dyke extended north from here to Bathampton Down where there is a hillfort. Colt Hoare thought he had also detected signs of the dyke in the grounds of Prior Park. With Maes Knoll at one end and Stantonbury in the middle of West Wansdyke, it made sense to look for another hillfort to anchor the eastern end. Bathampton Down, across the River Avon from the Roman Road, seemed logical. Indeed the 1926/9 revision of the 1" Bristol District Ordnance Survey Map shows the dyke leading northwards to the hillfort and a further short stretch running eastwards from the east bank of the River Avon opposite. This was probably Crawford's doing, as he was the archaeologist for the Ordance Survey at the time and supported the idea of a northward extension. He later changed his position over the presence of the dyke beyond Horsecombe Vale, citing inexperience as the justification for changing his mind (Crawford 1953 p253). The Foxes, as noted above, did not consider that there was sufficient evidence to justify a northern extension. The generally accepted view now is that the defensive or boundary line followed the course of Horsecombe Vale down to the Midford Brook which flows into the River Avon about a mile to the north east. Each of these features would have represented a significant barrier to an attacking force or clear boundary markers.

This is an appropriate time to discuss the role of the hill forts on the dyke since, with the exception of Chisbury, which may not part of Wansdyke anyway, it is the first time we have encountered them. Here, Maes Knoll and Stantonbury are key elements of the structure, while a further fort at Stokeleigh on the Avon Gorge has been proposed as the true western end point of West Wansdyke by Keith Gardner, and Bathampton was once proposed as the true eastern end point. As we will see later on, these hillforts were originally Iron Age constructions, so earlier than the time frame we are concerned with. However, there is evidence that they were re-occupied in the post-Roman period, and so could have been very much part of the planning and construction of the earthwork.

What evidence is there that the builders of Wansdyke incorporated the ramparts of the hillforts into their construction? The Foxes were convinced that there was no connection. They asserted that the dyke did not touch the Iron Age defences at either Maes Knoll or Stantonbury and that there was no gap in the inner fort defences to allow movement (Fox 1960 pp 27-8). Gardner has reviewed more recent evidence, which asserts, to the contrary, that both hill forts were integral parts of the dyke (Gardner 1998 pp60-1). At Maes Knoll, he notes that the Foxes considered that the dyke stopped short of the eastern rampart of the hill fort. Work by Rahtz and Barton (1963) and Tratman (1963) led them to the view that the dyke continued along the northern rampart of the hill fort to the large mound, known as The Tump, which effectively terminated the dyke. Burrows' resurvey of the fort in 1974 showed a termination of the dyke at the eastern rampart of the fort, as opposed to stopping short of it. At Stantonbury, the Foxes considered that Wansdyke was not constructed along the north facing hill slope and that, as at Old Oswestry hill-fort on Wat's Dyke, the Iron Age defences were deemed sufficient (Fox and Fox 1960 p32). However, Gardner asserts that the dyke runs right up to the ramparts on both sides of the camp. Confusion could have occurred because the Foxes mistook the fort for a univallate (single ditch) structure, when, in fact, it is multivallate (Gardner 1998 p60). The Foxes were seeking an Anglo-Saxon scenario for Wansdyke and this may have influenced their thinking. To my eye, the dyke seems to join to the ramparts of both hillforts, and the evidence cited by Gardner seems to favour them being an integral part of the construction.

Overall, West Wansdyke is something of a puzzle, both because of its discontinuity and because over much of its length it is in a very poor position for defence. What it does achieve, however, is the blocking of some major trackways, including, in particular, the Fosse Way, but also the Jurassic Way at Park Farm.

Considering the gaps first, The Foxes identified three places where neither air photography nor field work had succeeded in finding traces of the dyke. These were over Publow Hill for a mile from Cottles Farm to Knowle Farm; east of Englishcombe for two thirds of a mile to the Breach Wood valley (Padley Bottom) and, less certainly, for a quarter of a mile east of Pennsylvania Farm (Fox and Fox 1960 p37). They

View from Fosse Way looking west along the li

noted that these gaps did not coincide with a change in soil and that rivers or topography did not provide a satisfactory explanation as the dyke occurs in similar locations elsewhere. Their conclusion was that the gaps coincided with belts of uncleared woodland or land which had reverted to forest in post Roman times. They regarded it as significant that they occur on hill tops (this is questionable) (*ibid* p38). Sir Cyril Fox had proposed a similar theory in respect of Offa's Dyke, but it was felt subsequently that relatively small belts of trees could have been cleared relatively easily, by fire for example. The explanation could simply be that these represent unfinished sections, with perhaps the presence of woodland giving construction in the particular location a lower priority.

     In terms of the defensive merits of the line of the dyke, there are many places where it is in a valley with high ground to the north. This is in stark contrast to East Wansdyke, which mainly follows the northern side of high ground, giving it a good vantage point over the surrounding

Copse by Park Farm

f West Wansdyke (taken in 2011 before recent hedge planted)

countryside to the north. The gap between Cottles Farm and Knowle Farm seems to suggest a line which would have skirted the southern side of Publow Hill. A valley location is very evident south of Lye Hill between Compton Dando and Stantonbury. Although its line on the south side of Padley Bottom may be considered an obstacle to attack from the north, it should be noted that the opposite side of the valley is generally higher and would have offered a good vantage point to attackers from the north while blocking long-distance views for defenders to the south. Indeed, it is strange that the dyke runs so close to, and parallel with, the River Avon, which would have been the logical boundary for both defensive and demarcation purposes. Erskine suggests that the use of the word *'speculatores'* by the British cleric Gildas may have referred to watchmen along a frontier set slightly back from the acknowledged front line (Erskine 2007 p103). There are two reasons for doubting this explanation. First, The Romans, in their *limes,* the extensive boundary walls mainly on the continent of Europe, had a tradition of using rivers as boundaries, rather than constructing walls or ditches. The River Avon here would be of sufficient size to be at least as effective as the earth bank as a defensive structure and obviously as clear a demarcation line as one could wish for. Second, it seems crucial that Bath was on the north side of the line. The builders of Wansdyke, it seems, did not control Bath. It seems inconceivable that if they did they would have placed either a defensive structure or a boundary marker to the south of such an important site. We are therefore left with the Foxes' explanation. At the end of their section on West Wansdyke, they commented: 'The alignment of much of West Wansdyke is militarily weak, lacking visual control of the Avon Valley. It indicates that the builders were not wholly free to choose their position.' (Fox and Fox 1960 p45).

The Western Extension of Wansdyke

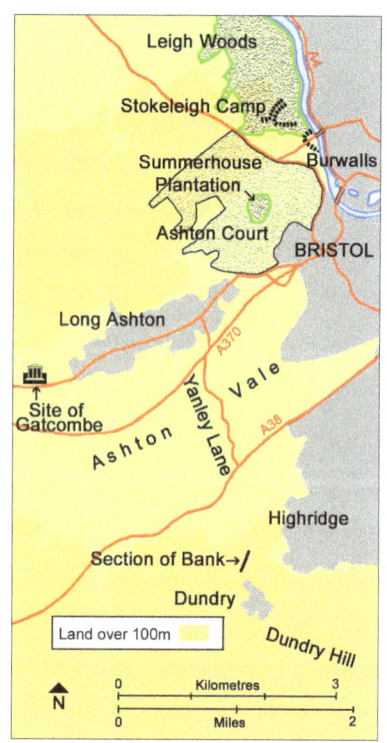

It always used to be assumed that Wansdyke carried on to the North Somerset coast of the Bristol Channel. William Barrett and Rev J Collinson in the 18th Century and Sir Richard Colt Hoare in the early 19th century all took this position, Rev Collinson stating that it 'terminates at the Severn Sea near the ancient port of Portishead' (Collinson 1792 Vol I p.xxiii). Major and Burrow in 1926 still showed this western section of the dyke with a branch extending up to Stokeleigh Camp on the edge of the Avon Gorge near what is now the Somerset end of The Clifton Suspension Bridge. By 1998, Keith Gardner, in his paper 'The Wansdyke Diktat? - A Discussion Paper' (Gardner 1998), was complaining that the Foxes had dismissed Major's fieldwork as ill-based and unreliable, and were adamant that Maes Knoll was

Suggested Western Extension to West Wansdyke. Contains OS data © Crown copyright Open Data 2011.

the western terminus of West Wansdyke. This is the 'Diktat' that he refers to. While the extension of Wansdyke to the Bristol Channel does not find any significant support these days, Gardner's paper explores the evidence for the extension of the dyke to Stokeleigh Camp. From here to the River Severn, the River Avon, and the famous gorge through which it flows, form a formidable barrier making any parallel extension of Wansdyke seem superfluous. In this section I will summarise his conclusions.

Gardner puts forward four pieces of evidence for consideration:

1. A large bank which descends the slope of Dundry Hill, the large hill running east-west across the south of Bristol, at its western end;
2. Two medieval charters which make grants of land in Long Ashton and refer to Yanley Lane, south of the village, as 'Wondesdich', together with possible archaeological evidence from a site in Long Ashton village;
3. Linear outworks to Stokeleigh Camp; and
4. A linear ditch in Summerhouse Plantation in Ashton Court.

The first reference to the bank is by Collinson, who was the vicar of Long Ashton in the late 18th century. He wrote of its course being 'directed hither from the ancient fortification at Mays-Knoll', a clear link to Wansdyke. He continues 'Descending the hill it crosses Highridge Common, where its tract is still visible'. Major also described the bank as exceptionally big but consisting partly of a natural ridge of rock. The bank, which is about 3 metres high and 170 metres long, is still very visible today, though there is not much sign of a ditch, which would be expected to be on the eastern side of the bank. Gardner notes that the oolitic limestone, of which Dundry consists, is notoriously prone to slippage, though the banks formed by this process on both Dundry and the Cotswolds are usually parallel to the slope. This bank is at right angles to it. He also notes that its scale is comparable to that on its descent from the north west corner of Stantonbury (see photo above) (*ibid* p59).

Yanley Lane is at the foot of the slope in Ashton Vale, the wide valley that runs between Dundry and the ridge which extends from Clifton to Clevedon on the Bristol Channel. It can be seen from the plan that the lane runs approximately north-south, and that if continued south it would lead directly towards Highridge Common. Again, it was Collinson who identified the existence of the charters that refer to the lane as *'Wondesdich'* or the *'venelle de Wondesdich'*, but they could not be traced for many years until they were eventually located in the Bristol Record Office. In the 1970s the two documents were photographed and Frances Neale translated them. Both date from March 1310 and describe 'Wondesdich' as one of the boundaries of the land in question. Neale also produced a sketch plan which shows the sites at the junction of the main road through Long Ashton and Yanley Lane. Gardner also quotes from Collinson, and Rev John Skinner's *Diaries* of 1830, which give further contemporary evidence of the use of the 'Wansdyke' appellation. Collinson says:

> . . . (Wansdyke) forms by its vallum a deep narrow lane overhung with wood and briars leading to Yanley Street in the Parish of Long Ashton. From Yanleigh it traverses the meadows to a lane anciently denominated from it Wondesdich Lane as appears from a deed dated at Ashton 3 Ed II . . .

Skinner's description from 1830 says:

> . . . I looked down upon Yanley Lane from a wall which bounds the road and perceived it ranged nearly into a straight line with High Ridge hill and Dundry tower. If this lane had been the course of the Wansdyke, . . . which the name seems to imply, for some of the people called it Wansley Street, it would have ascended the height near where I stood to make my sketch and there seemed to be a corresponding lane ascending the hill and pointing to the heights above.

Certainly, there is still today a public footpath which leads from the A38 opposite the end of Yanley Lane directly up to Highridge Common (Peart Hill). Gardner also shows that further evidence was produced by an excavation in advance of housing development in the 1980s at Lower Court Farm in Long Ashton. This uncovered a medieval settlement which had associated with it a linear feature described as 'a hollow-way or silted up boundary ditch' which ran north up the hill towards the main A370 road. He clearly felt that the failure to try to link this evidence to the medieval charters at the time was a missed opportunity (*ibid* pp 59 and 64).

Gardner felt that some sign of Wansdyke ought to have shown up in the Ashton Court Estate, which occupies much of the land between Long Ashton and Stokeleigh Camp, but there is very little evidence. The 340 metre linear rock-cut ditch in Summerhouse Plantation, described as a 'camp' in the 1917 Ordnance Survey map, is the only candidate he could identify (*ibid* p60). This shows up as a quarry in later maps, and this may be its correct origin. The line and location do not really fit the likely course of the dyke very well.

The final piece of evidence is an outwork to Stokeleigh Camp on the southern edge of the Avon Gorge. The camp is essentially double ditched but along its north western side is a third bank and ditch which turns abruptly west at the point where the inner ramparts turn south. It continues for about 50 metres with a break before petering out. Haldane speculates that the temporary disappearance of the rampart and ditch suggests that this portion was unfinished (*ibid* p60). The difficulty with attributing this earthwork to Wansdyke is that it wraps round the northern side of the camp, which would effectively leave the camp outside the defensive line and the ditch is on the northern side of the bank whereas it should be on the south to fit with the remainder of the proposed line.

The theory behind this extension makes perfect sense. No claim is made by Gardner for a defensive line along the top of Dundry, though Major proposed one. The hill is seen as a sufficient obstacle in its own right. However the remainder of the line in a sense completes Wansdyke. It takes it to the highly defensible boundary of the Avon Gorge, which in turn provides a defensive line running to the Bristol Channel/ River Severn. Secondly, it provides a defensive line across the highly vulnerable Ashton Vale. This provided access to two important sites, Gatcombe and Cadbury-Congresbury, either or both of which could have been a 'command centre' for a polity occupying north Somerset in the late Roman or post Roman period. Gatcombe was an important Roman site just to the west of the suggested line (*ibid* p 62). The hillfort of Cadbury-Congresbury is further away, but there is evidence for its reoccupation in the 5th century, which we will look at later

Gardner does not claim to have proved the case for a northern extension with this evidence, but he does argue that it raises questions to be answered, on which, no doubt, only further excavations can throw any light.

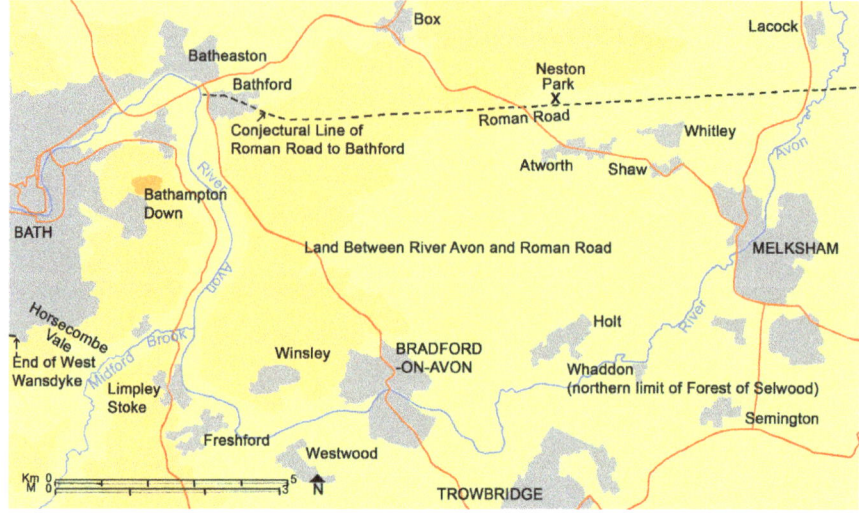

The line of the Roman Road from Bath to Lacock. Contains OS data ©
Crown copyright Open Data 2011.

The Missing Middle Section

In the past it was generally held that the Roman Road from London to Bath formed the middle section of Wansdyke between Bath and Morgan's Hill. We have already encountered this road at the western terminus of East Wansdyke at Smallgrain, west of Morgan's Hill. From here it runs in a nearly dead straight line to a point above Bathford just to the east of Bath. Moreover, it was built on a bank, known as an *'agger'*. It fitted the bill perfectly and, consequently, it was generally assumed that the road and Wansdyke were one and the same. At Sandy Lane, near Calne, the site of the Roman settlement of *'Verlucio'*, there is still a house on the line of the road called 'Wans House'.

Vermaat discusses the evidence of two medieval charters in his paper 'Wansdyke and the Roman Road' (Vermaat 2001). The first, originally identified by Robert Harvey, is from the medieval Cartulary of Shaftesbury Abbey, probably dating from 1122 or later, which relates to a land transaction on the Abbey's estates at Bradford-on-Avon. The landowner is described as holding *'a virgate of Wadenesdich for 6s'*. The

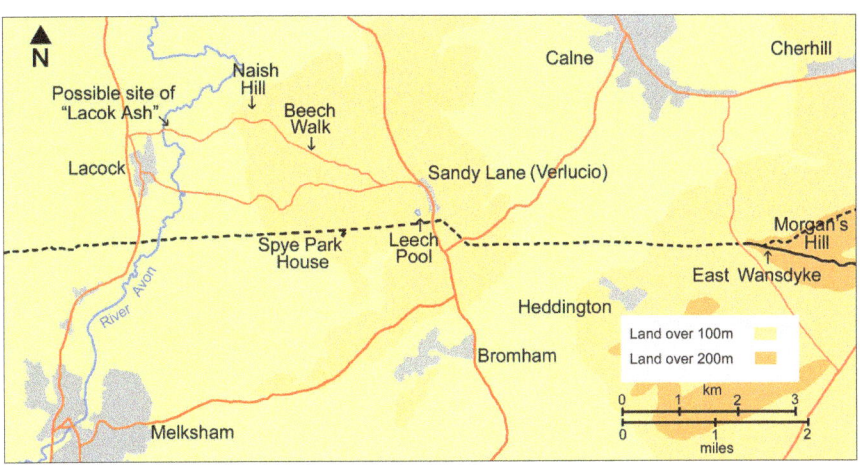

The line of the Roman Road from Lacock to Morgan's Hill. Contains OS data © Crown copyright Open Data 2008/2011.

precise location of the land is unclear but the reference is thought to be to Wansdyke. The parishes of Wraxall and Atworth belonged to Bradford at that time, and the northern boundaries of both parishes are formed by the Roman Road. For the second charter, Vermaat refers us back to an article by George Grundy from 1939 on 'The Ancient Woodland of Wiltshire'. In this article, Grundy identifies two references to Wansdyke in the description of the perambulation of Melksham Forest dating from 1300. Under Point 18: *'To Wodenes Ditch'*, he notes that this brings the boundary to a definite determinable point, the Wansdyke, at the place where the Chittoe parish Boundary coming from the south meets it at the west edge of Spye Park (Grundy 1939 p578). Under Point 19: 'Descending by the *Wodenes Ditch* to the Avon' he notes that the perambulation runs west along the Wansdyke to meet the Avon a little more than ¾ mile about due south of Lacock Village (ibid p579). It is thought that Grundy may not have realised at the time that what he had identified as Wansdyke was also the Roman Road (Vermaat 2001).

This demonstrates that the Roman Road was thought to be Wansdyke in antiquity, and it was only in the middle of the 20th century that any archaeological evidence was produced to determine the matter. The work was carried out over four digs between 1954 and 1957 by Tony Clark, reported in an article in *Antiquity*, 'The Nature of Wansdyke', in which he describes the digs.

Clark was puzzled by the line of the 'Middle Section'. He says:

> ...this line no longer follows hill ridges, and it connects awkwardly with
> the Somerset section; worst of all, it cuts across a great loop of the Avon
> where the River is well developed, and its defenders would have been
> isolated from the main part of their territory with all lines of retreat cut
> off by the River (Clark 1958 p91).

He continues:

> ... the dyke, it seemed to me, could far more logically be expected to
> continue approximately the line thus established by following the Avon
> upstream, than by indulging in a huge 3-mile jump and then pursuing
> a tactically bad course isolated from its main territory by the very loop of
> the Avon it seemed to run into so naturally (ibid p92).

To understand Clark's reasoning, it is necessary to understand the
nature of the gap between East and West Wansdyke, at least in broad
terms. It can best be thought of in three sections. The first of these
(starting from the west) consists of Horsecombe Vale descending to the
Midford Brook which then flows into the Avon, which we have already
looked at. Clark's point is that the location at which the Midford Brook
flows into the Avon is some three miles upstream of Bathford, the closest
point to the Roman Road. The Roman Road runs in a straight line from
a point above Bathford to cross the River again at the point described in
the perambulation of Melksham Forest ¾ mile below Lacock. Between
Bathford and Lacock is the second section. From Lacock, the River
flows in a large loop initially in a wide floodplain as far as Bradford-on-
Avon where it cuts through the southern fringes of the Cotswolds in a
steeply sided valley to Bathford. In this section the line of defence or
demarcation could follow either the river or the Roman Road. Finally,
the third section is from Lacock to Smallgrain where East Wansdyke
begins, and the Roman Road is the only option for a line.

Clark had believed that the loop in the Avon formed the central
section of the dyke, but he says he had to abandon this hypothesis
when he learned of Sir Cyril Fox's discovery of the termination of East
Wansdyke so far from the river at Morgan's Hill. This may have been

The 'agger' of the Roman Road from A342

premature. However, Clark's main work was not on this section but in Spye Park in the middle of the third section.

Spye Park is a large estate immediately to the west of the village of Sandy Lane. Here, Clark notes, the course of the Roman road had become defensively untenable. A much better line would have followed the Old Bath Road which ran along the northern side of the ridge. A belt of trees called Beech Walk and a narrow modern road fulfilled these conditions, and the road led to a promontory camp with a wide rampart and ditch, called Naish Hill, where he found Roman pottery (*ibid p93*). He resolved to carry out excavations on this alignment. In 1954 he sectioned the embankment on which Beech Walk was planted, but found it too insubstantial to be Wansdyke. In 1955 he cut across the Old Bath Road. A V-sectioned dark pocket in the sand caused initial excitement but proved to be a geological feature. He concluded that the Beech Walk-Bath Road alignment was a red herring (*ibid* pp93-94).

Sections were then cut in 1956 and 1957 in the Leech Pool field just inside the east wall of the park by Sandy Lane village 'to disprove the coincidence of the dyke and the Roman road in Spye Park'. The road *agger* is particularly high and impressive here. The sections were extended north of the road and a ditch was encountered but it was considered too trivial to be part of the dyke. Throughout the ditch he found fragments of charcoal and iron-blooming cinder that had spilled in from the north soon after the ditch was originally dug. Clark considered that these tell of peaceful activity alongside the road not a frontier line. Trial trenching to the south revealed no ditch either (*ibid* p94).

On the basis of these excavations, Clark concluded that the Roman road was not Wansdyke in the sense of the bank and ditch construction we see elsewhere. However, this does not rule out the use of the road as a boundary line, a function it could have served perfectly well.

Clark notes that supporters of a continuous Wansdyke (eg Colt Hoare) have tended to focus their attention on Neston Park, where the agger was of unusual height before being reduced for landscape reasons in the 19th century. A manuscript by Leman, transcribed by Colt Hoare, seems to show the road with a great bank piled upon it. However, Skinner, writing at the same time (1819) gives a pair of more detailed sections which show a more modest earthy layer overlain by small stones and gravel, consistent with an upgrade of the Roman road. (*ibid* p95).

Skinner's sketch of Roman Road in Neston Park

I referred to the abandonment of the hypothesis that the River Avon formed the defensive or demarcation line as premature. The reason for this is that the section between Lacock and Smallgrain/Morgan's Hill was probably part of Selwood Forest, a large tract of woodland running from the Dorset border up the boundary between Somerset and Wiltshire and on into Wiltshire, possibly extending as far as Braydon in north east Wiltshire (Clark 1958 p94, Eagles 2001 p220). Clark discusses this point, noting that Sir Cyril Fox had suggested to him that the commander of an ill-disciplined group of settlers could only have controlled his horde if it was in full view at all times (The Foxes reiterated this point in 'Wansdyke Reconsidered' p2). He also notes that the great ditches of the oppidae at Colchester and Bagendon, near Cirencester, exploit woodland in this way, while Caesar talks of surprise attacks by British cavalry from woodland in *De Bello Gallico* (Clark 1958 p95).

Selwood Forest seems to have been a serious tract of woodland. There are three references to it in Asser's *Life of King Alfred* and another in the *Anglo-Saxon Chronicle*. Asser, writing in 893, was Bishop of Sherborne, having been 'recruited' by King Alfred when he was still at St David's Cathedral as part of Alfred's drive to turn his court into a centre of learning and literature. The events Asser is referring to relate to a later period than the construction of Wansdyke. We therefore have to assume that the Forest had not changed greatly in the intervening period.

Asser describes a gathering of Alfred's troops prior to the Battle of Ethendune in 878 at a place called Egbert's Stone in the eastern part of Selwood Forest. He describes Selwood as *'sylvia magna'* (great wood) in Latin and *'Coit Maur'* in Welsh (Asser p84). Earlier, he had outlined a 'disgraceful episode' where a revolt against King Aethelwulf was fomented in the western part of Selwood (*ibid* p70). The third reference describes another gathering of the troops to repel the Vikings, this time in 893. The King's thegns are described as 'assembled from every burh east of the Parret, and both east and west of Selwood, and also north of the Thames and west of the Severn' (*ibid* p116). In this reference Selwood seems to be a location of some importance. This does not sound like some small patch of anonymous woodland, but a major geographical feature that separated sufficiently large areas of country to make such a reference meaningful and recognisable to the readers. The same is true of the *Anglo-Saxon Chronicle's* reference. This is a reference for the year 709, though, like Asser's work, it was written much later. It records the death of Aldhelm, the first bishop of the newly created diocese of Sherborne, and describes him as bishop of Westwood, also recognised as 'west of the wood' (*ASC* pp 40-1).

The Domesday Book shows that in the 11th century the area on the Wiltshire-Somerset border contained the biggest concentration of woodland south and west of London and the Home Counties (Rackham 2001 p49). Later, in Medieval times, Selwood became a series of Royal Forests. The main area retained the name Selwood, and covered the Wiltshire-Somerset border area up as far as Whaddon near Bradford-on-Avon. North of this were the Royal Forests of Melksham and Chippenham. We have already seen that the northern boundary of Melksham Forest was the Roman road. The Chippenham Forest perambulation, also of 1300, indicates that the two Forests were not quite coterminous. The southern boundary of Chippenham Forest is identified by Grundy as following the road from Sandy Lane to Naish Hill, then to the 'Ash of Lacok', impossible to locate now, but probably on the River Avon somewhere below Naish Hill, and then, probably up the River to the bridge at Chippenham (Grundy 1939 p580). Lacock seems to have been outside the bounds of the Royal Forests. However, a forest area continued in the medieval period to the north of the Roman road.

Selwood should probably not be seen as a tract of impenetrable wildwood. It is almost certain that in Roman and Post-Roman times wildwood had almost disappeared from the British countryside (Rackham 2001 pp 35 and 40). Asser refers to it as a gathering place, which is also not consistent with it being wildwood. The Romans had constructed at least two major roads through it: the Bath-London Road and another connecting the lead and silver mines at Charterhouse to Old Sarum and Winchester. However, we have seen that Wansdyke generally avoided woodland areas, with the exception of West Woods and possibly Savernake. We have the Fox's interpretation that woodland was difficult militarily and it was certainly true that the major requirements of a defensive boundary; to see and be seen, could not be fulfilled in woodland.

We will see later that Wansdyke may have been in active use for a very short period and Fowler's hypothesis that it was never finished. The explanation for why the middle section of Wansdyke is missing may be as pragmatic as it being of low priority and, consequently, they never got round to it. The existence of a combination of a large tract of woodland and the River Avon would have formed an adequate defensive line without the need for further earthworks. The Foxes note that it would be consistent with the established principles of a post-Roman linear earthwork that the loop of the river should have no defence, while hostile north to south movement in an area which was heavily wooded and, they claimed, sparsely populated, would be unlikely (Fox and Fox 1960 p2). If all that was required was a demarcation line, the Roman road fulfilled the condition admirably and would be the kind of feature that might well have been referred to in any settlement between two warring parties. This begs the question of which, if either, of the two alternatives actually reflected the situation at the time. We will probably never know.

There is a bigger question underlying this. If the middle section of Wansdyke is missing, are the two sections of the dyke part of the same structure or were they separate constructions which may have been built at different times by different parties? The Foxes subscribed to the latter view, stating that 'it is clear that Wansdyke can no longer be regarded as the remains of a single frontier and in consequence it is no longer necessary to search for a moment in time when a frontier was established in Britain extending from Inkpen to the the Severn . . . or Maes Knoll' (Fox and Fox 1960 p39). However, there are reasons for thinking that the two sections are part of one and the same structure. Firstly, the alignments of the two parts are very similar; they naturally form a single defensive or boundary line. It may be no coincidence that East Wansdyke connects to the Roman Road at its western terminus, if this was intended to be the continuation of the line. The reason that they do not reconnect at Bath may be due to difficult topography or the fact that Wansdyke's constructors did not control the relevant land around Bath (we already know that they did not control the city itself and therefore probably did not control the defensive routes to it, of which the area around Bathford would have been one). Secondly, within the limits of different ground conditions, the two stretches of earthwork are of sufficiently similar construction to suggest that they were both built by the same party, while the dating evidence, such as it is, is similar for both. Thirdly, they both have the same name in near contemporary documents. These are matters which I will discuss in more detail in Chapter 4 in which I will look more closely at the form and structure of the dyke from the archaeological evidence.

Conclusion

There is a consensus that there are two sections of Wansdyke; West Wansdyke stretching from Maes Knoll to the top of Horsecombe Vale and East Wansdyke stretching from Morgan's Hill to New Buildings west of Savernake Forest. It is generally accepted also that the Roman Road between Bathford and Morgan's Hill is not Wansdyke, but may have been used by the builders of the dyke as a ready made boundary. The River Avon between Bathford and Lacock could well have been used as a defensive line and this would be consistent with Roman practice elsewhere.

The source of controversy is over whether Wansdyke extended beyond the terminal points described above. The argument has been made by Keith Gardner for a north-westward extension of the dyke to Stokeleigh Camp, on the west side of the Avon Gorge, though the evidence is probably insufficient to prove the case. In the past, it was widely believed that West Wansdyke extended to Bathampton Down at its eastern end but the Foxes were of the opinion that it did not, and this idea has little currency today. Moreover, any evidence is probably now lost to development. An eastward extension of East Wansdyke as far as Inkpen on the Berkshire border has been a widely held view which is regaining currency, as we shall see.

3
Of Antiquarians and Archaeologists

Sir Richard Colt Hoare called it a quest. A hundred years later, Albany Major called his book *The Mystery of Wansdyke*. Wansdyke has fascinated and perplexed in equal measure for at least 350 years - probably much longer. Its very name, *Wodnesdic* - 'God's Dyke', suggests that 1100 years ago the people who gave it the name we know it by today may have had no idea who built it.

In the previous chapter we have already had our first introduction to many individuals from the cast of characters who have contributed to the body of knowledge that now exists about Wansdyke. In this chapter, I will look at some of these characters in more detail, in their historical context, from the early antiquarians to the highly technical archaeologists of today, explaining what each of them has brought to the party. This will then give us a platform to look at the archaeology of the earthwork, which will allow us to examine such questions as when it was built, why it was built, how it was built and what it may have looked like.

The Early Antiquarians
The earliest surviving reference to Wansdyke is genarally taken to be by the 16th-century antiquary, John Leland, described as the 'father of English Local History and bibliography'. Leland undertook a series of itineraries round England and Wales between around 1538 and 1545, keeping notebooks as he went, which were subsequently compiled into his *Itinerary*. This contains the reference to Wansdyke as being built to separate the kingdoms of Wessex and Mercia.

This theme was continued by John Aubrey, the 17th century antiquary, folklorist and biographer, who provides us with the first worthwhile description of the monument in his *Monumenta Britannica*. Aubrey was born at Easton Piers or Piercy to the north of Chippenham in 1626. One of his greatest claims to fame is the rediscovery of the stone circle at Avebury. Almost nothing of his work was published in his lifetime, but manuscripts were left in various libraries. *Monumenta Britannica* is Aubrey's main archaeological work, compiled over a thirty year period between 1663 and 1693. This was not published in book form until the 1980s, and it is fortunate that Colt Hoare had access to the manuscript and quoted extensively from it in *The Ancient History of North Wiltshire* of 1819.

Aubrey tells us:

> The middest of this shire (Wiltshire) which for
> the most part lieth plain and even, is divided

John Aubrey

> overthwart from East to West, with a dyke of wonderfull work, cast up
> for many miles together in length: the people dwelling thereabout call
> it Wansdyke, which upon an error generally received, they talk and tell
> to have been made by the Divell upon a wednesday: for in the saxon
> tongue it is called WODENESDIC, ie the ditch of Woden or Mercury,
> and, as it should seem, of Woden, that false imagined God and father of
> the English saxons, made it as a limit to divide the two kingdomes of the
> Mercians and the West Saxons asunder. (Colt Hoare 1819 p16).

Colt Hoare also quotes Aubrey's description of the Dyke, which he describes as 'limited'. Aubrey has it running from 'Spie Park to Milton' (which Colt Hoare identifies as Manton), adding that 'they say it runnes into Savernake Forest'. Aubrey identified that the bank or rampire was to the south and the ditch or graffe to the north, and referred to its 'prodigious greatnesse' (*ibid*).

Wansdyke also caught the attention of William Stukeley, the 18th century antiquarian who was famous for pioneering the archaeological investigations of Avebury and Stonehenge, which included attempting to date Stonehenge for the first time. Colt Hoare called him 'the literary restorer of our Wiltshire Antiquities'. His investigations at Avebury and Stonehenge must have made him familiar with Wansdyke, which featured in his *Itinerarium Curiosum* published in 1776, eleven years after his death. Here, he notes it as running from two miles south of Marlborough to 'the highest apex of Runway Hill', this being his name for Morgan's Hill.

It is not certain whether Stukeley was familiar with Aubrey's work, but from Colt Hoare's comments it seems that he might have been. However, he came to a radically different conclusion about the origins of Wansdyke, which became the accepted version of its origins for over a century, only being convincingly disproved by Augustus Pitt Rivers' dating evidence in the late 19th century. Stukeley's observations, in his words

William Stukeley;   . . . overthrow the notion of those that imagine Wansdike was cast up by the Saxons, as a limit of the West Saxon, and Mercian Kingdoms, or that its name is derived from the God Woden: but here we have a most incontestible proof that it was in being before the Roman times; and its very name shows it, signifying, in the old British language, the division dike; guahan, distinctio, separatio: It is, indeed, the work of the Belgae, their fourth and last boundary. . . Wansdike was made by the people of the south, to cover their country, as the mode of it sufficiently testifies; and, as we have said before, was the most northern bounds of the Belgic kingdom (Stukeley 1776 p142).

Stukeley identifies four boundary ditches which he attributed to the Belgae: Combesditch in Dorset, Bokerly Dyke on the Dorset/Hampshire border, ditches in South Wiltshire between Durnford and Newton and on Groveley Wood (probably Grim's Dyke) and finally Wansdyke, each being, according to him, constructed as the Belgae moved northward.

The 'incontestable proof' he refers to seems to be the intersection of the dyke and the Roman road at Morgan's Hill.

Soon after, it [The Roman road] meets with the Wansdyke' he says, 'descending the hill just by the gibbet: here it enters full into it, and very dexterously makes use of it, all along the bottom, on a very convenient shelf, or spurn of the hill: at the place of union is a flexure of the Wansdike, so that the Roman road coincides with it directly; and in order to raise it from a ditch into a road, the Roman workmen have thrown in most part of the rampire, still preserving it as a terrace to prevent the danger, and the terror of the descent on one side (*ibid* p142).

In other words, he believed that Wansdyke pre-dated the Roman road. In this he was deceived according to the Foxes (Fox & Fox 1960 p6).

The Belgae were the last people to invade Britain before the Romans. The events are chronicled in Caesar's *Commentaries on the Gallic War,* and are recounted by the Reverend John Collinson in his *History and Antiquities of the County of Somerset* in 1792. Here, he tells us that much of the south west from Middlesex to Cornwall was occupied by the Belgae, a brave Gaulish people, but of Celtic origin, who migrated out of Gaul in 313BC. About 250 years after their original settlement, Divitiacus, king of the Suessones, and according to Caesar, the most powerful prince in Gaul, brought over a considerable Belgic army to extend their territory. It was proposed that Wansdyke was the result of a treaty between the Belgae and the native Britons to define the boundary between them (Collinson 1792 Vol I p xxii). This would date Wansdyke to the first half of the first century BC, before the Roman conquest of Britain. This is consistent with the link to Divitiacus, said by tradition to be the founder of Devizes, to have had a palace there and after whom the town is named (Colt Hoare 1819 p28).

We have met Collinson before in the context of the eastward and westward extensions of Wansdyke, especially his original identification of the bank on Dundry Hill and the charter linking Yanley Lane at Long Ashton to Wansdyke. He was born at Bromham in Wiltshire, not far from the Roman road, in 1757. He had begun work on his history of Somerset in 1784 while living in Cirencester. In 1787 he was appointed to the living of Long Ashton by Sir John Smyth of Ashton Court. His parochial duties were not onerous and the preparation of the history probably took up most of his time. The three volume work was produced in 1791. It is still the only work of detail which includes every parish in the historic county of Somerset. Collinson died at Hotwells in 1793 after a lingering illness at the age of only 36. Collinson described the dyke as running from Andover to 'the Severn Sea near the ancient port of Portishead' (Collinson 1792 p xxiii). Apart from his suggestion that it extended to Andover, he very much reflected the received wisdom of the time.

A rather eccentric alternative was described by William Barrett, a surgeon from Bristol, who produced what might be thought of as a companion work to Collinson's history of Somerset, *The History and Antiquities of the City of Bristol*. This was published in 1789, slightly before Collinson's work, and again had been a long time in preparation. Barrett did not finish it until he had retired to the country from his practice as a surgeon in Bristol due to gout. Without naming it as Wansdyke, he describes a '*praetentura* or fence against any inroad or attack' which can be traced from the two camps of Bower-walls (Burwalls) and Stokeleigh 'proceeding in a nearly straight direction toward Fayland'. He continues:

> At every opening towards the vales and at every eminence where a distant prospect of the country around and of the river afforded an opportunity of descrying an approaching enemy, there circular watch-towers were raised, there the ruins of walls crossing the fence and outworks for garrisons, etc. still appear; the stones ranging in that manner loose above ground at this day. This fence may be traced all the way westward by the broad high stony bank for many miles skirting the hill, fronting the south and extending towards Clevedon and Walton, where there are now traces of camps marked out near the severn, which seems to have been its bounds;. . .
>
> There are vestiges also of a circular castrum on the brow of a hill opposite Nash House and near Failand Inn, about seventy feet diameter a castellet, and about three quarters of a mile farther eastward is a square fort or exploratory turret about seventy feet square. These were fortresses or chesters all garrisoned, attendant on the principal station of Clifton and Abone (Sea Mills), and the old roads from the camps on Leigh-down may be still traced through an orchard at the village of Leigh and through Leigh-wood down to the River Avon at Sea Mills (*op cit* pp19/20).

The fortifications described are clearly Roman in inspiration rather than Belgic, Somerset's own version of Hadrian's Wall, and the line described is well to the south of Collinson's line, following the Tickenham Ridge to Clevedon rather than terminating at Portishead.

Barrett's work is seen as the first attempt to produce a history of Bristol soundly based on documentary sources. However, his misfortune was to meet Thomas Chatterton, the solicitor's clerk and poet, who, over a period of months, supplied Barrett with a large number of forged documents containing completely fabricated information. Barrett seemingly accepted this information uncritically and incorporated it into his work. On a visit to Bristol in 1776, Dr Johnson immediately saw through the deception, but this seemed to have no effect on Barrett, who pressed on with his publication. When the *History* was published it was subjected to a long and highly critical review in the *Gentleman's Magazine* which exposed Chatterton's forgeries. Barrett was clearly stunned by this turn of events and it is considered that it contributed to his death shortly afterwards (Bettey 2003).

Consequently, Barrett's Wansdyke seems to have been quickly forgotten. Samuel Seyer, a Bristol schoolmaster and friend of Barrett's, produced a much more soundly based history of Bristol entitled *Memoirs Historical and Topographical of Bristol,* published in two volumes in 1821 and 1823. This made passing reference to Barrett's *praetentura,* suggesting that he did not think this to be one of Chatterton's fabrications. However, Colt Hoare included Collinson's description in the historical review of Wansdyke in his *Ancient History of North Wiltshire,* but made no reference to Barrett's work, which was now effectively discredited.

Sir Richard Colt Hoare

The name of Sir Richard Colt Hoare has cropped up time and again in this account. He was a leading antiquarian and archaeologist of his day and few would object to him styling himself 'the historian of Wiltshire'. He lived from 1758 to 1838, and inherited the large Stourhead Estate in south west Wiltshire in 1785 from his grandfather, Henry Hoare of the banking family C. Hoare and Co. This enabled him to travel and to pursue his archaeological interests. With William Cunnington, he excavated Stonehenge and many barrows on Salisbury Plain. He succeeded to the baronetcy in 1787, became a fellow of the Royal Society in 1792 and was high Sheriff of Wiltshire for 1805.

His importance for Wansdyke is that he produced the first full and systematic study of the whole earthwork. Given the breadth and depth of his knowledge and experience we can regard this as a reliable account. As such it is valuable to give us a snapshot of the earthwork at the turn of the 19th century. This is especially important for West Wansdyke, which has suffered from the ravages of ploughing much more than East Wansdyke.

Sir Richard Colt Hoare

I have noted Colt Hoare's descriptions of particular parts of the monument in the previous chapter where they throw additional light on its line and construction.

Colt Hoare's description of Wansdyke is contained in Volume 11 of his work *'The Ancient History of Wiltshire'*. This work is also in two parts, the first covering the pre-Roman period dated 1819 and the second covering the Roman period and beyond dated 1821. His description of Wansdyke is contained in the first part, since Colt Hoare subscribed to Stukeley's view that the dyke was a Belgic boundary dating to the first century BC. However, he also proposed that it had been added to by the Saxons for increased strength (Colt Hoare 1819 p17). Though his investigation of the dyke was restricted to fieldwork, he was able to view a section through it when a sheep drove was made. He describes it as follows:

> In the year 1817, a curious and very satisfactory discovery was made on the line of Wansdyke between Shepherd's Shore and Tan Hill, which evidently proved, that this agger was first raised to a certain height, and subsequently encreased in altitude. This important discovery was made by digging through the Wansdyke to make a sheep drove, when the evident marks of the first and subsequent agger were clearly visible, with the different strata of mould, chalk and turf The first probably raised by the Belgae, the last by the Saxons (Colt Hoare 1819 footnote to p29).

Colt Hoare describes West Wansdyke as extending from Maes Knoll to Bathampton, but expressed himself doubtful that it extended west of Maes Knoll. His friend Mr Leman and his surveyor Mr Crocker had minutely examined the ground and could find no trace. This included investigations of Bower Walls and Stokeleigh camps and Yanley Lane. We know that Colt Hoare was familiar with Collinson's work on Yanley Lane as he had been a subscriber to Collinson's book and summarised it in his description of Wansdyke. (Colt Hoare 1819 p21)

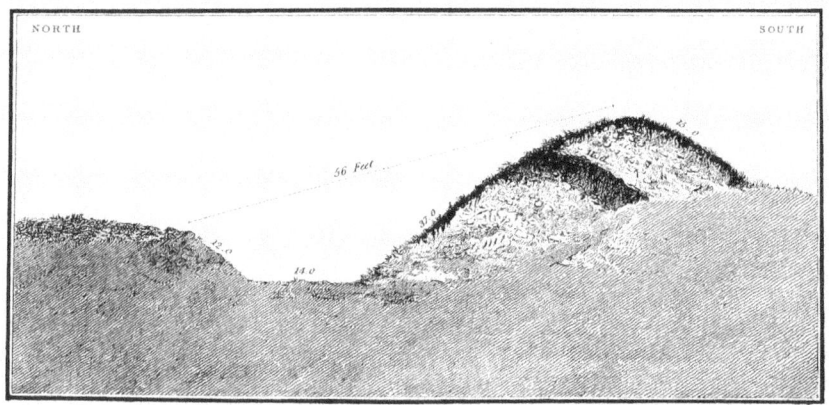

Colt Hoare's section near Shepherd's Shore

He was uncertain whether the Roman road between Bath and Morgan's Hill was part of Wansdyke. It looked to him like a Roman road not a Belgic or a Saxon boundary. However, he was convinced that a Saxon bank and ditch were plainly visible on top of the Roman road in Neston Park. It is Tony Clark who points us to Reverend John Skinner's sectional drawing of the bank at Neston Park published in 1820, which he claims demonstrates that the bank represented improvements to the Roman road rather than a later addition.

The sudden disappearance of the dyke 'at a spot near Ivy's Farm' perplexed Colt Hoare. Ivy's farm was adjacent to Wernham Farm, and Colt Hoare must have been referring to the location at New Buildings. He wondered whether the impracticality of building it through the thick forest of Savernake was the explanation. He talked it over with his friend the Earl of Ailesbury, a major landowner in the area whose estates included Savernake Forest. Ailesbury recalled a strong bank and ditch on one of his farms on the east side of Savernake Forest 'in a valley running north-south a little to the west of the 70th milestone on the London Road and south of Kembridge House'. Colt Hoare says that he recognised it as Wansdyke, and adds that 'A native shepherd recollected that it crossed the vale and ascended the hill towards the Great Bedwyn Road' (Colt Hoare 1819 p30). This spurred him on to find further traces of what he believed to be the dyke at Park Copse, 'Cheesbury' Camp, west of Prosperous Farm and Broad Lane Ditch at Inkpen. These are the same fragments of bank later examined by Crawford and the Foxes, with the Foxes concluding that they were not part of Wansdyke. However, Colt Hoare was convinced that the dyke extended to Walbury Camp. He anticipated finding traces further east in Berkshire and hoped to trace it to Silchester, but inquiries of 'the most intelligent inhabitants of the neighbourhood' yielded nothing (Colt Hoare 1819 p33).

Finally, we should note his view of the incorporation of the various hillforts into the construction. Maes Knoll, Stantonbury and Bathampton were 'evidently raised at the same period with the dyke and formed part of it', he says. At Cheesbury, however, he thinks the builders availed themselves of an older British camp (Colt Hoare 1819 p31). This theory made sense in the context of an earthwork built in the first century BC.

Reverend John Skinner

A number of other commentators from this period included descriptions of Wansdyke in various publications, without saying anything radically different from the contributions we have discussed. However, before leaving the age of the antiquarians, we should note the contribution of the Reverend John Skinner. We have noted his comments on Yanley Lane at Long Ashton and the Roman road at Neston Park. He was born in 1772 at Claverton, near Bath, and became vicar of Camerton, a few miles south of Bath, in 1800. He had a fixation with all things Roman, but especially Roman roads, which is surely the inspiration for his sketch of Neston Park. He was an irritable man and he suffered from depression leading him to commit suicide in 1839. He kept a series of journals, which are regarded as important historical

Rev'd John Skinner (Radstock, Midsomer Norton and District Museum Society, on display at Radstock Museum)

documents. He was one of the 'Two Parsons' in an essay of that name written by Virginia Woolf. His vision of Wansdyke, which he called the *Vallum of Ostorius*, was of a line of camps defending the area of North

Somerset he called Camulodunum, the name normally associated with
Roman Colchester. This line extended from Stokeleigh Camp to Frome
(Major and Burrow 1926 Appendix VI, quoting from Chapter III of
Skinner's *Memoir on Camulodunum*).

Skinner was an acquaintance of Colt Hoare, but we know that they
had a disagreement over the location of *Camulodunum*, as Colt Hoare
wrote at some length to the Bristol Philosophical and Literary Society
in 1827 on the matter. Skinner had presented his views to the society.
The preface to Colt Hoare's letter confirms that he disagreed 'in toto'
with his 'learned and reverend friend' and puts forward the evidence for
Camulodunum being Colchester (Colt Hoare 1827).

So we leave the age of the antiquarians with the received wisdom
being that Wansdyke was a Belgic construction built as a boundary
between them and the British in the first century BC, though Colt Hoare
did concede that the Saxons may have added to it.

Augustus Pitt Rivers

Nearly seventy years were to elapse after the publication of Colt Hoare's
'The Ancient History of Wiltshire' before Augustus Pitt Rivers carried out
his historic excavations on Wansdyke which produced the first, and
to this day, the most authoritative dating evidence for the dyke. Pitt
Rivers has been called the father of scientific archaeology. His scientific
thoroughness and his insistence that all finds be saved rather than just
unique and valuable artefacts set him apart from his predecessors. His
stated aim was to collect evidence that would stand up in a court of law.

He was born Augustus Henry Lane-Fox near Wetherby in Yorkshire
in 1827. He had a long and distinguished military career in the Grenadier
Guards, retiring in 1882 with the rank of Lieutenant-General. He had
developed an interest in archaeology and ethnology in the 1850s during
his time in the military, and was already a noted scientist while still a
serving officer. Two years before his retirement he inherited the estates of
a cousin, Henry Pitt-Rivers, 6th Baron Rivers, and with it a considerable
fortune. These estates were at Rushmore on Cranborne Chase on the
Wiltshire-Dorset border. Lane Fox adopted the name Pitt Rivers which
was a requirement of the bequest. From the mid 1880s until his death
in 1900, Pitt Rivers excavated many sites all over the country, including
many on or near his estates. He became the nation's first Inspector of

Lt-Gen. Augustus Pitt Rivers

Ancient Monuments in 1882.

Pitt Rivers was invited to dig Wansdyke by Reverend A C Smith, author of the then well known work *British and Roman Antiquities in North Wiltshire* and Secretary of the Wiltshire Archaeological and Natural History Society. He had heard of Pitt Rivers' excavations of Bokerly Dyke and thought that he was probably in favour of Wansdyke being of the same date, that is to say from the Roman or immediate post-Roman period. This must have caused some excitement in archaeological circles in Wiltshire, because it is clear from Pitt Rivers' own account that Stukeley's and Colt Hoare's theory that Wansdyke was constructed in the late Iron Age by the Belgae was still current, but now the evidence from Bokerly, if it were replicated at Wansdyke, would prove it to be much later.

Pitt Rivers was around 60 at this time. He says that he 'pressed upon Mr Smith the desirability of carrying out himself the investigation . . . which he had every claim to consider his own, but he explained that his health at the time quite unfitted him for the task.' Fortunately, therefore, Pitt Rivers was persuaded to undertake the work himself. He carried out a series of digs between 1889 and 1891 on East Wansdyke. These are recorded in his privately printed book *Excavations in Cranborne Chase, Volume III: Bokerly and Wansdyke*, which incorporates some beautiful engravings illustrating the sections dug and the finds.

The excavations at Bokerly Dyke had been begun in 1888, which is how Reverend Smith got to hear of them. These excavations provided a context for the Wansdyke excavations and gave important background which helped to date the Wansdyke finds. It is therefore relevant first to describe some of the most important features of that series of excavations and their relevance to Wansdyke.

Bokerly Dyke is another earthen bank and ditch construction of

Bokerly Dyke

similar proportions to Wansdyke, though much shorter. It forms the boundary between Dorset and Hampshire just south of the point where it meets the boundary with Wiltshire. It was thus very close to Pitt Rivers' home at Rushmore. The dyke runs approximately west and south east from the point, known as Bokerly Junction, where it crosses the Roman road from Old Sarum to Badbury and the modern day A354, which are within a few yards of each other at this point.

In digs lasting a total of about 5 months spread over 1888 to 1890, Pitt Rivers discovered a possible three different stages of construction of the dyke. What seemed to be the oldest section ran from the south east, stopping at a short return in the dyke which Pitt Rivers called an 'Epaulment' about 2000 feet (600m) south east of Bokerly Junction. The continuation to the north west was later, and was itself made up of two successive stages of construction which diverged at Bokerly Junction into what Pitt Rivers described as the 'Fore Dyke' and the 'Rear Dyke', the latter being the older. It is these later stages, which cross the Roman road, that Pitt Rivers was able to prove were Roman. In addition, he discovered a Roman settlement immediately to the north of the dyke to the west of the Roman road. Probably because of the proximity of the settlement, Pitt Rivers found a large number of Roman coins which enabled him to date the ditches with some precision, or, at least to determine the earliest date by which they could have been built.

In fact, he found 584 coins in the rampart and the silting of the Fore Dyke, dating from the period of Gallienus to that of Honorius (395-423), from which he deduced that this dyke must have been made at or after the departure of the Romans, which he dated to 407. Excavations

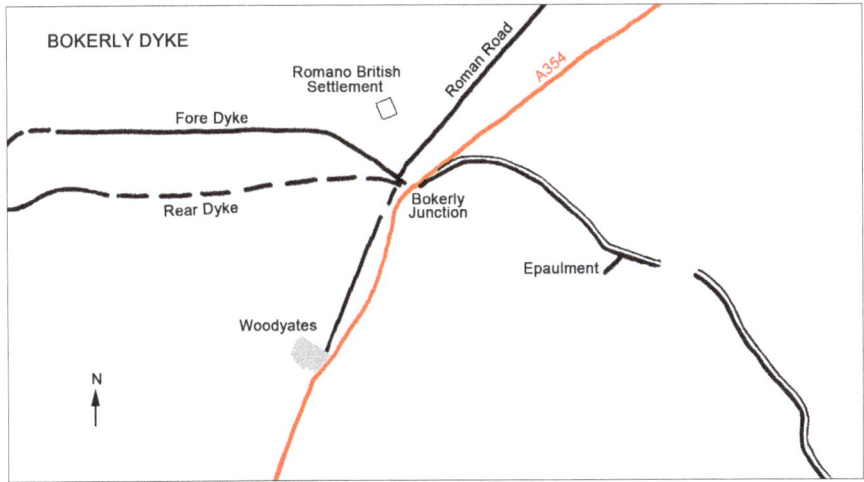

Pitt Rivers' Excavations at Bokerly Junction. Contains OS data © Crown copyright Open Data 2013.

along the Roman road showed that the Fore Dyke was built over the flint pitching of the road, while the pitching went over the filling of the ditch of the Rear Dyke. In other words, there had been activity at more than one stage of the Roman occupation which may have extended beyond the end of it. The Roman road cut across the Rear Dyke but was blocked by the Fore Dyke. Pitt Rivers suggested that the Fore Dyke may have been constructed by Romanised Britons as a defence against the Saxons, going as far as to propose that it could not have been built much earlier than the year 520 when the West Saxons under Cerdic and Cynric, after having taken *Sorbiodunum* (Old Sarum) advanced westwards to capture 'Mons Badonicus', 'supposed but not proved by Dr Guest to be Badbury' (Pitt Rivers 1892 pp 15-20 and 28).

In the settlement area a number of skeletons were found. One, with a Roman coin (a Faustina) under its chin, was surrounded by hob nails. Another had iron cleats and hob nails from shoes around it. These were the type of artefacts which were found at Wansdyke, and the dating evidence of the coins at Bokerly provided a vital context for dating them (*ibid*).

Pitt Rivers began his excavations at Wansdyke in 1889. He quartered himself at The Bear at Devizes, driving up the hill every morning, presumably in the carriage that he used on his digs in Cranborne Chase, so as to arrive at the time the men began work and returning every evening after the work was over (*ibid* p25).

Pitt Rivers' first excavation at Wansdyke was a massive 30 foot wide trench cut on a section of the dyke between Old Shepherd's Shore and Morgan's Hill. This resulted in the discovery of an iron knife and an iron nail 5.36 feet (1.6m) beneath the surface of the rampart. He considered that the knife might well be Roman though it would be difficult to be certain. He believed that nails such as the one found were not in use for fastening timber before the Roman conquest. Fragments of Samian pottery, that characteristic red Roman pottery, were discovered in the small outer rampart on the old surface line, indicating that this part of the dyke was of Roman origin. The fragments of Samian ware were of good quality with deep colour and glaze indicating that they were of a type made before the end of the 3rd century (*ibid* pp26/27).

However, he did not regard this evidence as conclusive, and so he returned in July 1890, this time to a location which he called Brown's Barn between Shepherd's Shore and Tan Hill. At this spot there is an ancient earthwork in the form of an enclosure which had been cut through by Wansdyke. He believed that the enclosure might be of earlier Roman date. He first cut a section parallel to the dyke in its outer bank. This was to investigate the relative ages of the dyke and the enclosure. He uncovered a section of the rampart with the ditch of the enclosure below it, thus proving that the enclosure pre-dated the dyke. A second section was cut through the dyke itself. This resulted in the finding of red Samian pottery on the old surface line, this time within the rampart of the dyke rather than the counterscarp. Pitt Rivers also found an iron cleat on the old surface line precisely similar to the cleats he had found at Bokerly Dyke. These formed part of the leather fastenings or sole guards of sandals. It is doubtful if he would have recognised it or

Pitt Rivers' Model of his excavations at Brown's Barn in Salisbury Museum (with kind permission of Salisbury Museum ©)

Photo of Pitt Rivers' Excavations at Brown's Barn
(reproduced by kind permission of Historic England)

been able to date it if he had not found similar ones *in situ* adjacent to skeletons at Bokerly and another site he had excavated on Cranborne Chase at Rotherley. As it is, these finds proved Wansdyke to be of Roman or post-Roman date (*ibid* pp 26/28).

He returned to Brown's Barn in 1891, when he dug a third trench across the rampart and ditch of the enclosure. He found nothing of significance. The interior of the enclosure was trenched in several places and more Samian pottery fragments were found. No coins were found. 'Under the circumstances,' he concluded, 'we are unable to fix the date of Wansdyke with the same certainty as that of Bokerly, although its Roman or post-Roman origin has been satisfactorily determined.' (*ibid* p 28).

It was the first time that trenches had been systematically dug through the earthwork and the results demonstrated how necessary this was in understanding the origins and history of the dyke. Pitt Rivers may have been less than totally satisfied with what he had found but, nonetheless, this was a huge step forward. For the first time it could be confidently said that the dyke was much later than had previously been thought, and the theory of its being Belgic, ie pre-Roman, in origin had to be discarded.

There was also the matter of Colt Hoare's hypothesis that the dyke, although originally built by the Belgae, had been reinforced by the Saxons, based on the dark seam he had seen in the cutting for the sheep drove. Certainly, Pitt Rivers' sections seemed to show a black line sloping upward through the front part of the bank to outcrop about halfway up its steeper, front face, giving every appearance of being the top of an earlier bank. The black line would have been mould caused by grass decaying, and Colt Hoare's interpretation was that this grass was originally on the top of an earlier embankment. Pitt Rivers went to some lengths to demonstrate that this was not the case. He produced elevations across his section, which showed that the seam was not continuous and in places dipped right down to the original surface line. He also pointed out that the seam was thicker at the top than the bottom, whereas, in his considerable experience, banks which have been overlaid with soil have less grass at the top than the bottom giving a seam which is thicker at the bottom than the top. Finally, he showed that the relics found above and below the seam were of precisely the same character. He explained the seam as being caused either by turf which had been cut from the ditch or by surface mould thrown up during construction (*ibid* pp252/3). As we shall see later on, he may for once, have been wrong on this matter.

Pitt Rivers reviews a number of possible theories for the construction of Wansdyke, without ever coming down in favour of any one of them. He also considers some of the more perplexing issues of the routing of the dyke. He suggests that Hadrian's Wall often goes behind hills as Wansdyke does at Morgan's Hill. Commanding a view was of less value in ancient times than now because the range of missiles is now so much increased. It was only necessary to command an area within 100 yards of the wall and this, he says, was never neglected. He also suggested that where the line runs through woods it may have been replaced by an *abattis* of felled trees, no trace of which now remains. It is to be observed that the rampart diminishes in size or is wanting in places where forests may have existed (*ibid* pp245/6).

Pitt Rivers' thorough approach has stood the test of time. His dating evidence is still relied upon after all this time and all the advances that have taken place in the 130 or so years since he carried out his excavations. It is fortunate that these excavations were carried out by someone so thorough and so knowledgable about these types of earthworks. Another archaeologist might well have missed the nails or the iron cleat or not understood their significance.

It is, perhaps, fitting to conclude this section on Pitt Rivers by quoting the final sentence of the main part of his report. This was of its time, and was a vigorous defence of seemingly unspectacular investigations of British antiquities as opposed to headline grabbing digs in famous locations abroad. He says:

> But in my judgement, a fragment of pottery, if it throws light on the history of our own country and people is of more interest to the scientific collector of evidence in England, than even a work of art and merit that is associated only with races that we are remotely connected with. (*ibid* p30).

It was typical of the man that he wanted to communicate this as widely as possible. He regularly commissioned 3D models of his digs, one of which was of Brown's Barn. He housed these in a museum in the village of Farnham in North Dorset, along with the often seemingly mundane finds from the digs, all clearly labelled. The Salisbury Museum now holds this collection, from which the photographs of the Brown's Barn model and the iron cleat are taken.

The Mystery of Wansdyke
A collaboration between the archaeologist, Albany Featherstonehaugh Major and the artist Edward J Burrow, *The Mystery of Wansdyke* was

the first book to deal exclusively with Wansdyke. It was published as a limited edition in 1926, the year after Albany Major died.

In truth, Major was the main driving force behind the project. He had first begun investigating the dyke in 1913 and 1914, recommencing work after the First World War. He also wrote most of the text. He described his method as starting with known sections of the dyke as shown on the 6 inch Ordnance Survey maps of the day. He would then examine the line or lines of continuation that looked most promising on the map and on the ground, and to search along these for indications of an earthwork. This was a very substantial exercise, representing probably the most comprehensive study of the dyke since Colt Hoare. Burrow, meanwhile, contributed a huge number of excellent water colours, illustrating every section of the dyke as he saw it. These were reproduced in black and white in the book, and a selection of them appears on the Wansdyke 21 website. Burrow also had to complete the book after Major's death and his own company in Cheltenham published it.

Along the way, Major had published 'The Course of Wansdyke Through Somerset', an article in the *Somerset Archaeological and Natural History Magazine* in 1924, which described some excavations undertaken during the investigations. As we have already seen, Major was also involved in Brentnall's digs at New Buildings and Savernake Forest in 1923 and 1924. Most of the work, inevitably, was confined to fieldwork however.

Major's conclusion was that Wansdyke was a composite work, made up of sections belonging to different periods and varying in size and construction, which were subsequently linked together (Major and Burrow 1926 p135). His vision of the dyke extended from the Bristol Channel at Portbury Island, an island where the flat land of Portbury Wharf is now located, through to Dundry Hill and Maes Knoll, with a branch extending to Stoke Leigh. From there he envisaged it extending to Bathampton Down before descending to the Avon and joining the Roman road opposite. He was an advocate of the link to Inkpen but also of the branch to Ludgershall, near Andover, although Burrow expresses his doubts about this latter section in his introduction to the book.

Major also explored the various theories for the origin of Wansdyke. He was clearly not convinced by the Saxon boundary theories, noting that there was never a time when the whole of the south side of the Dyke was British and the whole of the north side Saxon (*ibid* p141).

The Mystery of Wansdyke should be a key work in the canon of literature on Wansdyke, but its reputation has subsequently suffered. The problem is that Major was a creative individual who was fond of lateral thinking. Whilst this should be a good thing, all too often two and two could end up being five. I am mindful of his theory, contained in *The Early Wars of Wessex,* that Alfred's great victory over the Danes at Ethendune in 878 was fought at Edington near Bridgwater, in Somerset, rather than Edington in Wiltshire, where everyone else considers it to have happened. Herbert Brentnall observed that 'Mr Major . . . assures me that Wansdyke is capable of many disguises' (Brentnall 1924 p74). O G S Crawford, on the other hand, declared that 'Albany Major's *Mystery of Wansdyke* is entirely untrustworthy. He had no eye for earthworks and mistook modern field banks for the remains of Wansdyke' (Crawford 1953 p252). Sir Cyril and Lady Aileen Fox endorsed Crawford's position, observing that 'A four page appendix by the late O G S Crawford in his *Archaeology in the Field* in 1953 contributed more to its understanding than 140 pages of Albany Major's obscurities' (Fox 1960 p1) . In the same vein, Tony Clark was dismissive of 'limitless misguided detail' which Major had used to justify his extensions of the dyke to Portbury and Ludgershall, which according to Clark, do not stand up to archaeological scrutiny (Clark 1958 p 91).

It must be recognised that this criticism was of its time. In the 1950s, Crawford, Clark and the Foxes all produced work that has been highly influential in shaping views on the nature of Wansdyke, and their views on many of the key issues, especially where the earthwork started and finished, did not coincide with Major's. It is to this work that I now turn. But before leaving Major, I have learned that, when it comes to Wansdyke, it is never wise to dismiss views that do not accord with the mainstream out of hand. Major may have got many things wrong, but not everything, and some of the issues he raises are still relevant today.

The 1950s - Wansdyke Reconsidered

Perhaps it was a new enthusiasm for archaeology after the Second World War was out of the way, but important work was carried out in the 1950s culminating in Sir Cyril and Lady Aileen Fox's study *Wansdyke*

Reconsidered, which was originally published in 1958 and is still highly influential today.

Earlier in the decade, O G S Crawford had published two pieces of work that featured Wansdyke. The first was a general archaeological work called *Archaeology in the Field,* referred to by the Foxes. It drew on Crawford's experience both at home and abroad, and contained an appendix specifically devoted to Wansdyke. This does not tell us anything particularly new about the earthwork, but it is significant that he should choose to devote a whole section of the book to it. The second was an article in the 1953-54 edition of the *Wiltshire Archaeological and Natural History Magazine* dealing specifically with the east end of Wansdyke, which we have already examined. These publications were produced after Crawford had retired from his job as the first Archaeology Officer for the Ordnance Survey. Osbert Guy Stanhope Crawford was born in India in 1886. He was brought up in London and Hampshire and educated at Marlborough College, where he may have first become acquainted with Wansdyke. He became the Ordnance Survey's Archaeology Officer in 1920, a post he held until his retirement in 1946. Here, part of his job would have been to advise on the naming of antiquities on Ordnance Survey maps, and we have noted that he changed his position on some of this advice with regard to Wansdyke, especially in the Bath area, as his experience developed. Perhaps this experience led him to be highly critical of Albany Major's inability to distinguish Wansdyke from field banks. In the latter part of the First World War he was an observer in the Royal Flying Corps until he was shot down and held as a prisoner of war until the end of hostilities. This must have been instrumental in his interest in the use of aerial photography as an aid to archaeology. He was a pioneer in this field. In 1924, he produced *Air Survey and Archaeology* which was published by the Ordnance Survey and in 1928 he collaborated with Alexander Keiller on *Wessex from the Air.* We have already seen that he supplied Herbert Brentnall with aerial photographs of the area west of Savernake Forest to assist his excavations in 1923. This would have been cutting edge practice at the time.

Tony Clark's work on the Roman road in Spye Park was carried out in the middle of the decade. At the start of his four year series of excavations he was only 24 years old. At this time he was also involved in developing the Martin Clark resistivity meter and he was a pioneer of geophysics. We have discussed his work in some detail in the previous chapter. Since this proved the absence of Wansdyke on the Roman road it does not help us to understand the properties of the earthwork so, while acknowledging the unique and important contribution which Clark made to the study of Wansdyke, further discussion here is unnecessary. However, Tony Clark retained a lifelong fascination with Wansdyke and his name will crop up again in this story.

The previous chapter is peppered with references to Sir Cyril and Lady Aileen Fox's work *Wansdyke Reconsidered*. This was a landmark in the study of Wansdyke.

Cyril Fox was another of those connected with the study of Wansdyke to have a local connection. He was born in Chippenham in 1882. In his youth he undertook a number of jobs. This led to him working part time for the University of Cambridge's Museum of Archaeology and Anthropology. He published a PhD Thesis on the archaeology of the Cambridge region in 1922 which had looked in some detail at the Cambridgeshire Dykes. In 1924 he was appointed curator of archaeology at the National Museum of Wales, and in 1926 he became the Museum's director, succeeding Sir Mortimer Wheeler in each of these posts. He remained director until 1948. He was knighted for services to archaeology in 1935. Aileen Fox was 25 years his junior, being born in 1907. She had become interested in archaeology after graduating in English at Newnham College, Cambridge. She became Cyril's second wife in 1933, and was a distinguished archaeologist in her own right.

Sir Cyril had produced what became the standard work on Offa's Dyke while at the Museum of Wales. The fieldwork for this was carried out virtually from the time he was appointed to the Museum as Wheeler knew of his work on the Cambridgeshire Dykes. He knew quite a lot about big ditches. The opportunity to reevaluate Wansdyke occurred when he was invited to lead a summer school at Urchfont Manor in Wiltshire in 1955 and subsequently to give the O'Donnell lectures at the University of Oxford. This had involved a visit to Wansdyke at Morgan's Hill. The Foxes realised that it offered a challenge and the need for a fresh approach. Accordingly, they started a programme of systematic fieldwork and research, which was partly funded by a grant to Aileen Fox from the University of Exeter (Fox & Fox 1960 p1). Unlike Cyril's previous work on the Cambridgeshire Dykes and Offa's Dyke, this was a collaborative effort between him and Aileen. This was perhaps necessary because Cyril was by now in his seventies .

Wansdyke Reconsidered was published in the *Archaeological Journal* in 1958 and subsequently reprinted as a stand-alone booklet in 1960. It is based on extensive fieldwork and research carried out between 1955 and 1957, but did not involve any excavations. It has become a benchmark for the study of Wansdyke. In the previous chapter, I have quoted extensively from what it has to say about the line of Wansdyke and the points at which the various sections start and finish. In this chapter and the next, I want to look at what it has to say about the structure of Wansdyke, what it was for and when it may have been built.

With regard to the structure of the dyke, the Foxes noted that the section on the chalk downland between Morgan's Hill and Wodensdene was built on a formidable scale, bigger than anything comparable except Devil's Dyke in Cambridgeshire - bigger than Wat's Dyke, Offa's Dyke or Bokerly Dyke (*ibid* p20 – the Foxes' comparative measurements can be found at pp47 and 48). The steep slope is in the region of 30 - 35° on the front face, and the length of the inclined bank that would have to be traversed by an attacker exceeds forty feet (12m) in places (*ibid* pp 22 and 25). The change of scale east of Shaw House is quite sudden, occurring over a distance of 300 yards, and reflects a change in the soil. They concluded that on the chalk downland Wansdyke was conceived and constructed as a military barrier, whereas on the clays it was built as a territorial boundary (*ibid* p23). West Wansdyke is much smaller than the higher sections of East Wansdyke on the chalk, but it compares with the scale of the sections on the woodland claylands east of Shaw House (*ibid* p38).

On the basis of Pitt Rivers' sections at Morgan's Hill and Brown's Barn, they noted no signs of sods or timber being used as a revetment, nor of cresting or a palisade. The top of the rampart is rounded and there are no surface indications elsewhere to suggest that it was designed or used as a patrol track (*ibid* p25). On West Wansdyke, at locations where the dyke had been cut into or ploughed over they saw no signs of stone revetment (p38). This, they considered, was the best defensive position for a people who had lost control of or who were denied control of the Avon Crossing (*ibid* p36). There was therefore some ambivalence on the Fox's part as to whether the dyke was built for defensive purposes but it clearly represented a territorial boundary. The importance of controlling the main routes that crossed it was also noted.

Having carried out no excavations they were not able to add to the dating evidence, except in two respects. First, their work on the junction of the Roman road and the dyke at Morgan's Hill demonstrated clearly that the dyke had been built after the road, not before it as Stukeley had thought. This work was carried out with the help of Desmond Bonney, then of the Royal Commission of Historic Monuments in Salisbury (*ibid* p 1). Second, on the basis of Pitt Rivers' Morgans Hill section, they concluded that the bottom of the ditch was probably flat floored, in contrast to Bokerly Dyke where the ditch is V-shaped in the Roman manner. East Anglian and Mercian dykes, which are Saxon, have flat ditches. Wansdyke, they concluded, was thus an intermediate form between the known examples of Romano-British and Anglian construction (*ibid* p25). This latter conclusion has been thrown into doubt by later work. Their work on fixing the ends of the sections of the dyke also led to the key conclusion, which we discussed in the previous chapter, that the two sections of Wansdyke were separate.

Unsurprisingly, therefore, they produced two different theories for when the two sections of the dyke were constructed and who by. They considered that it was improbable that such a sacred name as 'Wansdyke' would be given by the Saxons to an obsolete defence of their British enemy. Accordingly, they sought a pagan-Saxon context. For East Wansdyke, they suggested that it was built by Ceawlin, the West Saxon king, after his defeat at *Woddesbeorge* in 592. This would have given him eight years to build the dyke, according to the chronology of the Anglo-Saxon Chronicle, and it would have been a short-lived construction, since in forty years the West Saxons, under Cynegils, were back in control of the area (*ibid* p 43). Aileen Fox sheds some further light on this suggestion in her autobiography. She describes how an old friend, Dr Kenneth Sisam, had drawn their attention to the poetical, heightened language of the Anglo-Saxon Chronicle when describing Ceawlin, which tied in with their view that the area around *Woddesbeorge* was a sacred precinct. She says that 'though well aware of the difficulties and uncertainties of correlating early history and archaeology, we bravely stuck our necks out, and tentatively identified Ceawlin as the builder of East Wansdyke in the sixth century.' (Fox 2000 p 122). With regard to West Wansdyke they suggested that, if it is of British origin then the obvious occasion would be after the battle of Dyrham or *Deorham* in 577. However, they preferred a pagan-Saxon origin here also. They argued, on the basis of the discovery of an inhumation cemetery at Camerton on the Fosse Way, a few miles south of Bath, that there was Saxon occupation of the north Somerset area by the early 7th century. The occasion when a defined frontier south of the Avon might have been needed would have been after the battle of Cirencester in 628. There were then seven years of paganism in which the dyke could have been built (Fox and Fox 1960 p 43). For those unfamiliar with these characters and events, I will be telling their story in Chapter 5.

Sir Cyril Fox died in 1967. Lady Aileen Fox survived him for 38 years. During this time she continued to work in Exeter and New Zealand. Her obituary notice describes her as 'probably the last surviving member of a generation of archaeologists who shaped the modern discipline in this country' (*Guardian* 20 January 2006). Certainly, after 1960, archaeology was becoming much more scientific. In the remainder of this chapter I want to examine three pieces of archaeological work from this period which have given important new insights into the understanding of Wansdyke, and are the reason why, some sixty years after it was published, a further reconsideration of the Foxes' work is now appropriate.

Stephen Green at Red Shore and New Buildings

Stephen Green, of the University of Cardiff, undertook a series of excavations at Red Shore and New Buildings on East Wansdyke between 1966 and 1970. These are reported in the *Wiltshire Archaeological and Natural History Magazine* of 1971. Examination of pollen analysis was an important objective of these digs, indeed the excavations at New Buildings were partial and designed solely for this purpose. The aim of this analysis was to investigate the nature of the agricultural uses which pre-existed Wansdyke.

At Red Shore, trial trenches were dug followed by a main section. Celtic fields underlie the Dyke and were certainly in use in the late first century AD. After the cessation of farming the area became pasture until the construction of the dyke, as evidenced by pollen samples of grasses, bracken and other plants associated with rough pasture. The bank was of a simple dump construction about 9.5 metres wide and just under 2 metres high. The ditch was always V-shaped, in contrast to the Foxes' observations, and was originally 3.9 metres deep, making a total height of just under 6 metres, or about 22 feet, from bottom of the ditch to the top of the bank. No evidence of palisading or revetment was found and there was no evidence of more than a small berm between bank and ditch. Turf from the surface of the ditch was not used in the bank but was added only late in its construction as a mull layer on the south slope. Normally, it would be expected that turf might be used to stabilise the bank, but its use on the south slope suggests otherwise in this instance as it would be the steeper north slope that would be more in need of stabilisation.

Any crossing of the ditch would need to be oblique as the ditch would need to be dug to a point slightly beyond the end of the bank to maintain its full height. (This may explain Brentnall's narrowing of the ditch at New Buildings, the ditch perhaps not being extended beyond the end of the bank). An original crossing might then have to be set obliquely to the ditch on one side of it only, and the Red Shore/Ridgeway crossing may be precisely of this type. Resistivity surveys, carried out by Tony Clark in what must have been cutting edge technology for the time, suggest that the causeway at Red Shore is original.

Finds from Red Shore included a Samian rim sherd from the first trench, which was identified as South Gaulish from about 80-100 AD, and three sherds thought to be Savernake or Broomsgrove pottery also from the first century AD. Other pottery fragments were more difficult to date. Ken Annable of Devizes Museum is reported to have examined the pottery 'and comments that he believes it to be Roman although he is far from certain.' A pennanular brooch, which could be from the Iron Age onwards, was also found (Green 1971 p136). These finds are of a slightly earlier date than those found by Pitt Rivers but are not inconsistent with them in respect of establishing a date for the dyke's construction.

Excavation took place at New Buildings in 1967. The picture painted by pollen samples of pre-existing uses is much more complex than at Red Shore. There is evidence of three distinct layers. The representation of woodland is high, whereas it is virtually non-existent at Red Shore. The interpretation is that the site was open but there was abundant

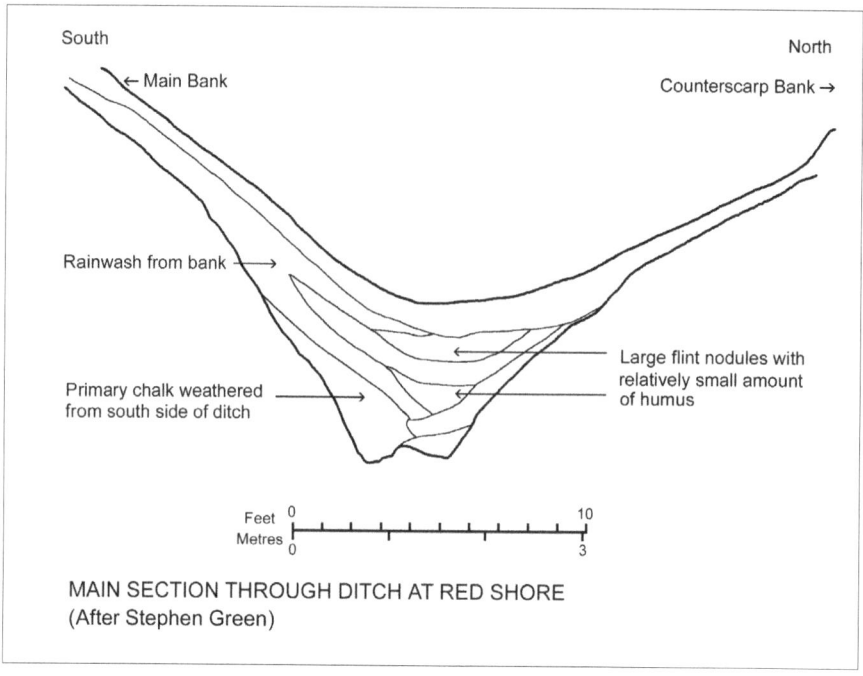

MAIN SECTION THROUGH DITCH AT RED SHORE
(After Stephen Green)

Simplified Section of Wansdyke at Red Shore (after Stephen Green)

woodland nearby. Characteristic plants of pasture are less prevalent, but there is some evidence of arable farming, though this may be short lived. The bank may have been built across derelict land. There is no evidence of topsoil being reserved for later use in construction of the bank, as at Red Shore, but a clay bank would need no such stabilisation (*ibid* pp 140-141).

Perhaps the most interesting hypothesis to emerge from these investigations was that the use of the dyke may have been very short lived. Layers of large flint nodules with relatively little humus were found near the bottom of the ditch close to the layer of silt from the bank. The flint and humus was thought to arise from clearance of the land north of the dyke being deposited in the ditch, and this would not have happened until after the dyke ceased to be in active use. The fact that the layer is so low in the ditch and associated with the silt suggests that filling in of the ditch started at a very early date after construction. A duration for the length of active use of Wansdyke of as little as five years is suggested, though this is also recognised as very much a minimum (*ibid* p134).

In parallel with the excavations, Green also discussed the relationship of Wansdyke to parish boundaries, based on a study being carried out by Desmond Bonney, indeed Bonney had an input to the article. Green noted that 'one of the remarkable features of the Wansdyke is the way in which modern parish boundaries bear almost no relation to it.' (*ibid* p141). These boundaries may have very early origins, and the behaviour of the dyke suggests that it postdates the boundaries which it crosses. He also suggested that this added weight to his hypothesis that the dyke was short lived as otherwise boundaries would have eventually reestablished themselves along the line of the bank (*ibid* p141). We will consider this evidence in more detail in the next chapter.

Green concluded that the Wiltshire Wansdyke consisted of two parts, joining at Shaw House. West of this point it was a military barrier but within a few years it had lost its military purpose. To the east it was probably a territorial boundary. This follows the Foxes' reasoning. In contrast to the Foxes, who proposed Ceawlin as the builder of Wansdyke, he proposes that it was a Cerdicing frontier designed for defence against Ceawlin, who, he argues, was a West Saxon prince from the Thames valley. He may have turned his attentions south on the West Saxons advancing northwards through Wiltshire, ie the Cerdicings named after their leader, Cerdic (see chapter 5), after the battle of Deorham in 577. A *terminus ante quem* would have been the battle of *Wodnesbeorg* in 592 in which Ceawlin was defeated. The name *Wodnesbeorg* is taken to imply the prior existence of Wansdyke.

Peter Fowler - Wansdyke in The Woods

In the previous chapter we looked at what Peter Fowler's study of Wansdyke in the Woods told us about the line of Wansdyke and the numerous gates that appear in this section of the dyke. The number of gates occurring close together is unlike any other section of the dyke (except perhaps an eastern extension into Savernake Forest). Fowler postulated that the purpose of the gates was to funnel north-south movement into this part of the dyke but then to facilitate and control that movement with a series of gates, arguably far more than were strictly needed. In this pattern he detected the precedent of Hadrian's Wall although the nature of the actual structures, one a stone wall the other an earth bank and ditch are very different. In this chapter I want to look at what Fowler says about the construction of this part of the dyke and his view of why it was built.

His was a fieldwork study, with no excavations, carried out in 1997 and 1998. It was published in *Roman Wiltshire and After - Papers in Honour of Ken Annable* in 2001, but drew heavily on work already published in 2000 in his *Landscape Plotted and Pieced,* a detailed study of Fyfield and Overton Parishes which are crossed by the earthwork. It represents the only detailed examination of Wansdyke east of Shaw House where it changes its character and becomes much smaller in scale. Brentnall's excavations were at and beyond the eastern end of the dyke while Green's excavations at New Buildings were partial for the purpose of collecting pollen samples only. Neither examined this particularly distinctive section of the dyke.

Fowler's distinctive conclusion was that this section of Wansdyke was unfinished. He detected a bank in various stages of construction, and he used this evidence to postulate how the bank was constructed. The stages are each illustrated by the earthworks in different parts of West Woods.

The first, most incomplete section is found between gates 7 and 8. Here, there is a 70 metre gap in the earthwork. Fowler describes a slight scarp running across the gap, falling about 30cm to where the ditch should be but is not. He concluded that it was a marking-out line for the bank which was never covered over because the bank was never built (Fowler 2001 p183). This marking-out line was clearly an important stage in the dyke's construction because it was where its line was initially established, using military criteria such as field of view and defensive qualities of the terrain, and also, presumably having regard to the boundary of the territory they were seeking to defend. This was his first stage of construction. The second stage, detected, for example, immediately to the east of the gap, consists of a series of shallow quarry pits, initially well in front of the marking out line, dumping the spoil on to the marking out line to begin forming the bank.

East of Gate 5, Fowler describes the bank as 'a series of dumps which have joined together in line but still show their own tales fanned out at the back. Each heap is 2-3m in width but not more than 0.5-0.75m high - hardly a mighty earthwork.' (*ibid* p182). He noted a berm on the shoulder of the original ground surface where the ditch and bank did not yet form a continuous slope. The original bank was even lower than it appeared because it was overlaid by a boundary bank for the copse, which undulated over the top of the bank. This represented the third stage. Fowler describes the third stage as looking as if the dyke was awaiting another one or two heightenings and a final smoothing out to complete the bank - the fourth stage, which can be seen for example between gates 8 and 10.

It can be seen that in the West Woods section we have a bank varying in height from as little as 0.5 m to nearly 2 m, but nowhere is it as high as on the downs to the west. The typical ditch dimensions are a width of about 6-7 m and a depth of about 1m. In places the ditch disappears to nothing, but it was beyond the scope of Fowler's study to determine whether it had been subsequently filled in or was never there in the first place.

On the basis of this construction model, and using experimental work that he had been involved in during the mid-1990s on Overton Down together with an engineer's estimates for the vallum behind Hadrian's Wall, Fowler concluded that the section of Wansdyke in the woods might have taken 1000 men about 20-30 days to complete (*ibid* pp192-3). Of course, we have no idea how many men may have been involved in the enterprise, but it is possible that, if sufficient resources were directed towards the project, it could have been built fairly quickly. If it was a defensive structure it would need to be, as its construction could be seen as a provocative act.

The proposition that Wansdyke in the Woods was incomplete has two important ramifications. First, it ties in well with Green's conclusion that the use of the dyke was short lived. It never became established as a boundary of any description in the longer term. As Fowler puts it, contrasting it with Bokerly Dyke, which remains the boundary between Dorset and Hampshire, '. . . Wansdyke left no imprint in either woods or minds. That it was referred to Woden, meaning its namers clearly had no idea who built it or when or why, speaks volumes about the brevity of its career and local significance.' (*ibid* p 195-6). Second, if it was not complete here, then it is logical to assume that it was not completed elsewhere. This could explain the gaps in West Wansdyke or the lack of a middle section. They were lower priority sections which the builders never got round to. This is consistent with a short lifespan for the dyke and suggests that whatever threat it was built to withstand became irrelevant, either because it went away or because the builders were overwhelmed before they could finish the project.

Fowler also gives a detailed description of the gateways. The two most complex are Eadgardes Gate and Titferth's Gate, where outworks in front of the dyke channel those approaching the gate in an oblique fashion. The alignment of bank and ditch are also staggered as part of the design of the gate. At Eadgardes Gate the ditches extend beyond the termination of the banks to narrow the access, while the outworks have almost disappeared from subsequent use. At Titferth's Gate, the constriction on the width of the track is provided by the banks. Here, the outworks can be clearly seen today.

Fowler proposes that the 'gates' may have been more than gaps in the dyke; they may have been, or were intended to be, actual gated structures. As on Hadrian's Wall, they may have been built as free standing structures to which the earthworks later abutted, but he considers it more likely that, in the case of Wansdyke, the bank came first, possibly with 'specialist gate builders' coming along later to complete the work (*ibid* p193). If the gates were timber structures, as seems likely, no trace would be left of them. Again, as with Hadrian's Wall, the purpose of the gates would be to

Titferth's Gate Looking South East

control movement not to prevent it. This begs the question as to whether they were used to charge tolls. Some of the gates may have been created by some design requirement rather than actual need, in order to have a regular series of gates, using Hadrian's Wall as a precedent.

This Roman inspiration is the basis for Fowler's hypothesis for the date of construction for the dyke. The scenario for East Wansdyke is that it was built in the late 5th century against an imminent invasion of Saxons from the Thames Valley. Such an invasion, Fowler proposes, would have to come down the line of the Ridgeway route to enter the heartlands of the still Romanised chalk country. A battle, Mount Badon, which Fowler argues might have been at Liddington Castle above Badbury Village near Swindon, or at Bath, proved decisive in that it halted the Saxon advance for a couple of generations. According to Gildas, a generation of peace followed. Its decisiveness was recognised immediately leading the builders of Wansdyke to down tools at once. As Fowler sums up: '(in the woods), at least, it is an earthwork firmly in the Roman tradition in thought, word and deed, built by Britons and nothing to do with the Saxons who failed even to arrive for its opening.' (*ibid* p 197).

The West Wansdyke Project
The West Wansdyke Project was a joint venture between the Avon Archaeological Unit and English Heritage designed to investigate the date, construction and route of the West Wansdyke. It was the first concerted effort to investigate the West Wansdyke using excavations, with the work being carried out in 1996. An account of the main findings appears in Jonathan Erskine's article in the *Archaeological Journal* for 2007 entitled 'The West Wansdyke: An Appraisal'.

A full programme of field walking and observation identified forty sites for geophysical investigation, either on the monument or its suggested course. Eleven sites were then selected for excavation. Only five of these sites produced any significant evidence:

Binces Lane East, north of Stanton Prior - site 1;
Binces Lane West, also north of Stanton Prior - site 2;
Compton Green, east of Compton Dando - site 4;
Blackrock Lane, Publow - site 9; and
Park Farm, Newton St Loe - site 10.

The excavated sites are shown on the attached plan. This also shows a location at Fairy Hill, which Erskine had investigated previously and describes briefly in his article.

It can be seen straightaway that there was a blitz on the area around Knowle Farm and Slate Lane/Wooscombe Bottom to the west of it, to try to find evidence of the dyke in the elusive Publow Hill Gap between Cottles Farm and Knowle Farm. None was found, indicating that the gap is real, not simply the result of ploughing out or other damage. On the other hand, evidence of the dyke *was* found at Binces Lane and east of Park Farm in locations where it is no longer visible. The site at Blackrock was a location where the bank is still evident and enabled its structure to be investigated.

The dimensions and profile of the ditch were found to be remarkably consistent along its length, the dimensions varying between about 5m and 5.4m wide and about 2.2m deep, being slightly deeper and wider where it was cut into softer natural sediments. At the Binces Lane sites, where the ditch was cut into rock, it was only about 4-5m wide and 1-1.5m deep. However, Erskine notes that the bank had largely been destroyed by ploughing and the dimensions of the ditch might also have been reduced. The profile was typically V-shaped, with in some cases a drainage channel or similar feature in the bottom.

The dimensions of the ditch could be assessed with greater accuracy than the bank because its outline could be detected in the trenches cut. Where the dimensions of the bank could be discerned, at Blackrock Lane, Compton Green and Fairy Hill, its width was typically in the range 12.5-14m. The height was more difficult to assess. Where the bank is best preserved at Blackrock Lane it was about 1.7m high, but Erskine suggests an original height of 2-3m with a ditch of similar depth, making combined vertical obstacle of up to 6m (Erskine 2008 p101). The banks were constructed with material from the ditch except at Compton Green where a section of imported yellow clay was evident. A counterscarp on the north side of the ditch was normally present.

All the bank sections, including sections at Compton Green and Stantonbury dug by Peter Fowler in the 1970s, revealed complex stratigraphy, suggesting that the dyke was built in   stages. This was most noticeable at Blackrock Lane, where two darker layers of

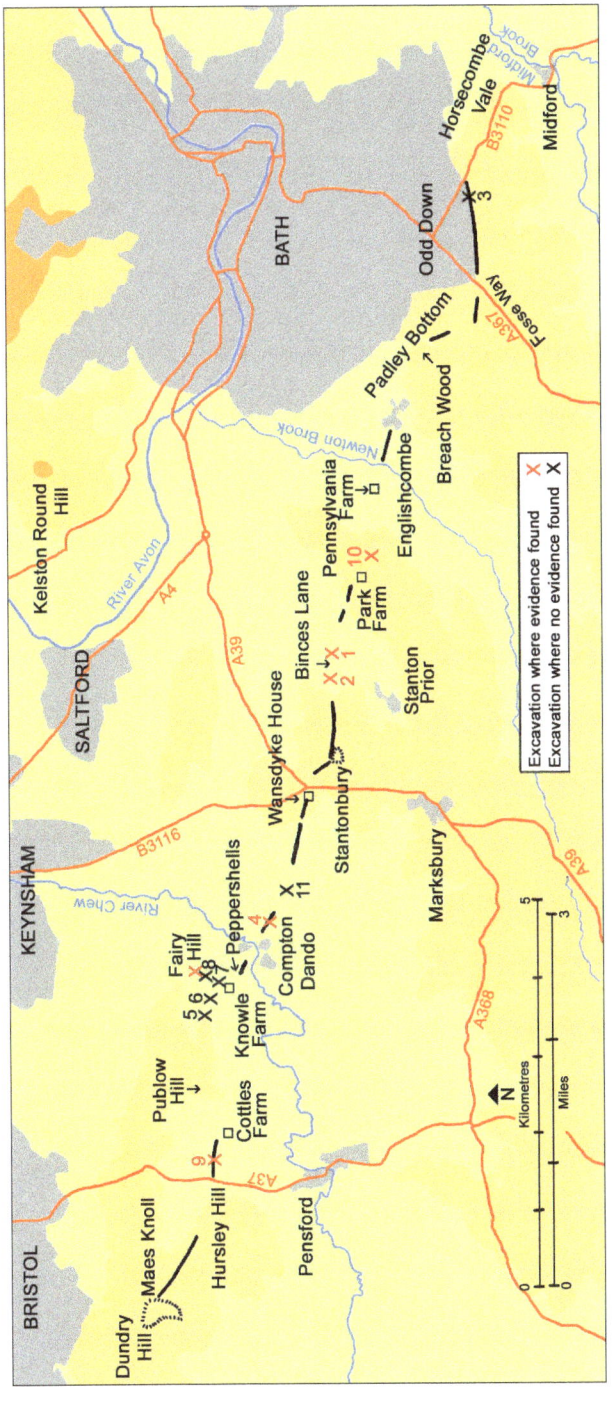

Location of sites in West Wansdyke Study. Contains OS data © Crown copyright Open Data 2011.

greenish-grey silty clay were identified. Each layer was of fairly consistent thickness (though both tapered to the south), and were interpreted as either carefully laid turf layers or as representative of periods when topsoil and/or vegetation was able to develop (*ibid* p91). As Erskine points out, the existence of layers seems to imply that the bank was not constructed in a single effort but periodically, perhaps over a number of years (*ibid* p104). Where the stratigraphy was well preserved the layers sloped uniformly at about 20° to the south creating an asymmetrical bank. This implies a pattern of deposition where ditch material was dumped behind a retaining structure. Foundation trenches were detected beneath slumped bank deposits at Blackrock Lane and Compton Green which were thought to be the foundations for a revetment probably of timber. Limestone rubble in the ditch at Binces Lane, some of which was found lying en echelon appeared to be derived from a collapsed stone-faced revetment structure (*ibid* pp 85 and 97). This is in contrast to East Wansdyke where no evidence of revetments has been found.

A longitudinal section at Blackrock Lane revealed that the internal layers were inclined at a steeper angle than the pre-existing ground level. This suggested that the preliminary stages of construction involved dumping excavated ditch material to form a series of heaps, which were then filled in to form a continuous bank, much as suggested by Fowler in West Woods. Alternatively, the bank may have been progressively extended in one direction by dumping material behind successive sections of revetment (*ibid* p 97). A survey of 294m of the surviving bank at Blackrock Lane was carried out to test this theory, which identified dumps at intervals of on average 24m. (*ibid* pp97-8).

At Binces Lane West a second ditch was found on the south side of the bank. This was a shallow, flat-bottomed, rock cut ditch, which contained

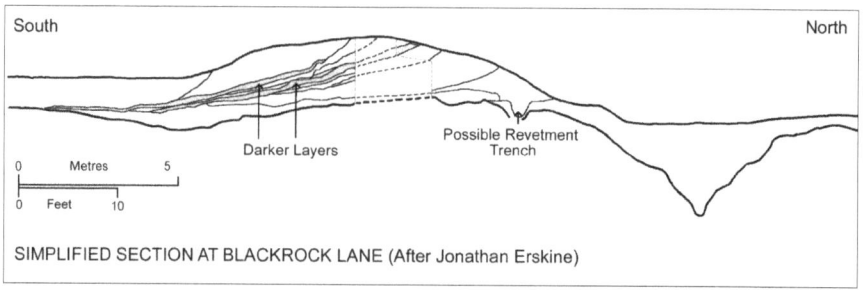

Simplified Section of Wansdyke at Blackrock Lane (after Jonathan Erskine)

a group of possible post settings in its base and side. The narrowness of the remnant bank deposit coupled with the curved and shallow nature of the southern ditch suggested an arrangement previously observed as an earthwork terminal elsewhere along the route of West Wansdyke, for example at the eastern termination of the bank at the River Chew at Compton Dando. The proposition is that the ditch was curved round the south side of the bank to provide more material to raise the height at its terminal. A dyke terminal in this position was previously unknown.

The Project confirmed that there were gaps in the dyke other than possible 'gates'. Besides the Cottles Farm to Knowle Farm gap, no evidence of a ditch was found at Goss Plantation near Compton Dando (Site 11) or Knowle Farm (Site 7). The assumption is that a ditch is necessary to provide the bank material, and that there may therefore have been no bank at these locations. This could be explained by other forms of barricades at these locations or that, if they were simply never completed, the construction team may have left the most difficult or least vulnerable sections till last. This might include wooded sections as suggested by Pitt Rivers and the Foxes (*ibid* pp 101 and 104).

Remarkably few artefacts were found during the project. The most significant of these fell into two categories. Fourteen pieces of struck flint were identified as being within the time horizon of late Mesolithic to early Bronze Age with a preference for early to middle Neolithic. The other category consisted of a relatively small number of pottery sherds in a poor state of preservation. These were difficult to date but were thought to be of generic prehistoric or Romano-British date. There was sufficient evidence to support the generally held view that the monument is Romano-British or later (*ibid* p94). However, this, together with the stratification of the bank, offers the intriguing possibility of the dyke being built on an earlier structure. Further evidence of earlier activity was found in the carbon dating of charcoal fragments at the base of the east-west section at Blackrock Lane, which dated them to 1000 to 520 cal. BC at 95% confidence (*ibid* p92). Perhaps Colt Hoare was right after all about the bank being built in two separate stages. Erskine certainly considers this a possibility, but one which will require further analysis to elucidate (*ibid* p101 and 105). We will consider this subject further in the next chapter.

Pollen samples at Binces Lane and Blackrock indicate that the dyke was built over arable land, or possibly pasture in the case of Blackrock, with the incidence of tree and shrub varieties being very low. However, tree and shrub pollen increases significantly in the secondary ditch fills, suggesting a period of scrub and woodland regeneration shortly after the abandonment of the dyke (*ibid* p94-5).

Like Fowler, Erskine produced an estimate of the rate at which the dyke might have been constructed. His source material was Roman technical military handbooks by Hyginus and Vegetius and *Military Antiquities of the Romans in North Britain* by General William Roy, the eighteenth century surveyor whose work led to the creation of the Ordnance Survey. From this material Erskine deduced that a standard 'dump' length of 24m (see analysis of Blackrock above) would require some 500m³ of material, probably, he says, less than a week's work for a gang of four experienced men equipped with iron tools in easy excavating conditions. This works out at about 18m³ per man day if a seven day week is assumed. He contrasts this with Fowler's estimate which he calculates to be equivalent to 4 to 5 m³ per day but notes that this includes women and children. The most likely method of construction would have involved small work gangs piling up sections of bank behind a stone or timber revetment, subsequently engineering it into a smoothed bank (*ibid* pp 98-9).

In seeking to date and provide a context for the dyke, Erskine also looks to Roman precedents, providing an analysis of other dykes and historical references to them. This is a theme that I want to return to in more detail in the next chapter. Suffice it to say here that Erskine follows Fowler's conclusion that the dyke was firmly in the Roman tradition. He comments that

> . . . Fowler's conclusion that the East Wansdyke was a fifth-century construction in a solid Roman tradition, but never finished, also seems to fit the new excavation data from the West Wansdyke. However, it remains a serious consideration that, at whatever date the West Wansdyke was constructed, the builders, in the interests of both expediency and economics, re-used much earlier prehistoric hillforts and possibly also Bronze Age ranch boundaries to form at least part of the monument (*ibid* p 105).

Conclusion

Our quest has taken us through 350 years of investigating Wansdyke and searching for an explanation for why this spectacular monument is there. I have not examined all the contributions to the debate over the years, but what is striking from this overview is that still we do not have clear cut answers to its origin. Modern excavations are now enabling a more systematic approach to the problem, but Erskine raises two difficulties which still lie in the way of finding answers. First, up to now, archaeological techniques have been insufficiently accurate to date mounds of earth that cannot easily be placed in a cultural context. Second, none of the literary sources for the period have been proved to be sufficiently reliable to provide that cultural context (Erskine 2008 p80). So each commentator has their own theory as to the origin of the dyke.

Early antiquarians such as Leland and Aubrey, saw it as separating Wessex and Mercia. Stukeley and Colt Hoare opted for Belgic construction in the first century BC while Barrett and Skinner proposed a Roman Wall. Only Colt Hoare proposed later, Saxon additions. Though Pitt Rivers ruled out this two stage process, the West Wansdyke Project brings the idea back into contention. Over the past fifty years, with modern archaeological techniques to back them up, scholars have tended to focus on two theories. One, favoured by the Foxes and others, is that it was a Saxon structure or structures, possibly built at different times by the West Saxons in the late sixth century. The other is that it was built by the British as a defence against the early advances of the West Saxons in the late fifth century. More recent attempts to find the cultural context for the dyke have led to the view that it is in fact the product of conflict between Romano-British polities which resurfaced during or just after the break-up of the Roman Empire in the late fourth or early fifth century. Now, as we shall see, we may be coming full circle, as a Wessex-Mercia boundary is firmly back on the table.

This speculation is fuelled by the fact that, for a monument of such a large scale relatively little dating evidence has been found. However, the huge body of work that has built up around the dyke does tell as a lot about it. In the next chapter I want to look at a number of themes that come out of this and other work, from which we can define the important characteristics of the dyke including its scale and construction and what purpose it fulfilled. Then we can go on to look at who built it and when.

4
The Archaeology of Wansdyke

Introduction
A self-contained archaeological site can be complex enough, but when the site is 21 miles long the difficulty of investigating it is raised to another level. Moreover, as a boundary feature it is by its nature removed from areas of activity, except those directly related to its own functioning (as with the forts along Hadrian's Wall and, perhaps, the hillforts on the West Wansdyke). It is these areas of activity, such as settlements and the workshops and cemeteries associated with them in particular, that provide so much of the dating evidence that archaeologists rely on. These are generally absent from Wansdyke, which is why so little dating evidence has been forthcoming. In the last chapter we traced a long history of studies of Wansdyke, each of which gives us only a small picture of the whole. Some studies reinforce each other and some contradict others. What is striking is how little firm evidence we have to tell us what the earthwork is about.

In this chapter I will build up a picture of Wansdyke from the many studies that have taken place over the years, starting with a description of the earthwork itself, examining why it may have been built, and briefly looking at the many other linear earthworks that appear to date from around the same time. Then I will look at the various pieces of dating evidence that we do have.

Form and Structure
As part of their study, the Sir Cyril and Lady Aileen Fox, assisted by Desmond Bonney, produced numerous profiles of the dyke along its length together with measurements. These were important to examine the extent to which it was a homogeneous structure and any variations along its length, given that the profiles were of the dyke as it existed in the 1950s when they carried out their study. They, indeed, relied on Pitt Rivers' sections and Colt Hoare's verbal descriptions for some of their

WEST WANSDYKE

EAST WANSDYKE (West of Shaw House)

EAST WANSDYKE (East of Shaw House)

TYPICAL SECTIONS

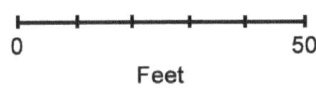

0   50

Feet

Wansdyke – typical sections from 'Wansdyke Reconsidered'

conclusions. The West Wansdyke project of the mid-1990s was also sufficiently comprehensive to draw generalisations about the earthwork. Clearly, any such conclusions about the dimensions of the dyke have to engage in a degree of projection about what it may have looked like when originally constructed. As we have already observed, this is easier with the ditch because the outline can be seen in the soil. In the case of the bank a degree of speculation is inevitable. These sources do suggest a considerable degree of consistency of character along the length of the dyke, which indicates a considerable level of pre-planning. In fact, we can divide the dyke into three parts, each of which is reasonably consistent along its length.

1. West Wansdyke (from Maes Knoll to Combe Down)

The ditch is typically about 4 - 5 metres wide and 1 - 1.5 metres deep. The bank is typically 12.5 - 14 metres wide and up to 1.7 metres high. Erskine suggests an original bank height of 2 - 3 metres and a similar ditch depth, making a total obstacle of up to 6 metres (almost 20 feet) vertically (Erskine 2007 pp 95 and 101). This conclusion would seem to need a degree of caution as the ditch profiles do not seem over-generous to supply sufficient fill for the bank as found at present in places such as Blackrock. Erskine suggests that the ditch was originally deeper, but he has nevertheless produced some remarkably consistent profiles for it. The Foxes estimated the rampart as originally standing 6 - 7 feet (1.8 - 2.1 metres) high (Fox and Fox 1960 p37). The earthwork also includes a counterscarp on the north side of the ditch.

There is evidence in several places that the bank was revetted along its north face by various means: stone, timber or turf. This could have been an aid to construction and would also have made the bank more difficult to scale. The ditch is mostly V-shaped, while the bank has a much steeper north face than its south face. As we have seen from the work of the West Wansdyke Project, it exhibits evidence of being built up in sections behind the revetment.

2. East Wansdyke from Morgan's Hill to Shaw House

This is the grandest section of the dyke where it crosses the chalk downland. Here, the Foxes recorded the width of bank and ditch together as being typically between 62 feet (19 metres) and 92 feet (28 metres) with a maximum width of 130 feet (40 metres). They recorded the bank as being typically 10 feet (3 metres) above present ground level, with maximum recorded heights in two places of 15" 6' (4.7m). However, the height above ground level can be deceptive when the bank is on a slope, as the accompanying sections show. These measurements are probably an underestimate of the scale of the original earthwork, which would have represented a formidable obstacle. A counterscarp was generally present, though it had been ploughed away in some places. In the most vulnerable places the counterscarp had been reinforced with fill from

Wansdyke at Morgan's Hil

a second ditch to the north (Fox and Fox 1960 p23). They found no
evidence of turf or timber being used as a revetment or of a palisade.
Their evidence for the ditch profile and dimensions is less helpful as they
undertook no excavations themselves and found Pitt Rivers' sections to
be 'unsatisfactory' in this respect (*ibid* p25).

Green assessed the dimensions of the bank at Red Shore to be
9.5 metres wide and 2 metres high. The ditch was always V-shaped and
originally 3.9 metres deep and 8.9 metres wide. He found no trace of
palisading or a revetment. Turf was only added late in the process on the
south slope of the bank.

3. East Wansdyke from Old Shaw House to New Buildings

As the Foxes note, the height of the earthwork diminishes noticeably
over a 300 yard stretch at Old Shaw House. Here, they estimated the
typical overall width to be about 50 feet (15 metres), with the bank
rarely exceeding 20 feet (6 metres) in width and 4.5 feet (1.4 metres) in
height (*ibid* p23). Fowler put the height of the bank at between 0.5 and 2
metres. He estimated the typical ditch dimensions to be a width of about

Wansdyke in West Woods

6 metres and a depth of about 1 metre. In the section through West
Woods the dimensions were extremely variable depending, as Fowler
asserts, on its degree of completeness (Fowler 2001 pp 182 and 186).
The Foxes found no trace of a counterscarp here. No excavations have
taken place in West Woods which might tell us more about the bank's
construction. Certainly, the method of construction described by Fowler
does not involve the use of a revetment.

　　These changes in character can be easily linked to the nature of
the ground crossed by the dyke. The chalk downland between Morgan's
Hill and Old Shaw House was sufficiently easy to work that larger banks
could be constructed and less support was required during construction,
which would explain the absence of revetments. A turf covering could
have been all that was needed, and Green suggests that not even this was
incorporated on the potentially less stable north face of the bank at Red
Shore. This must allow the possibility that on this section of the bank the
white of the chalk was deliberately exposed to add to the grandeur of the
dyke. Off the chalk, construction was more difficult, such that the scale of
the bank was slightly less and more use was made of revetments.

Gaps

There are gaps along the length of the dyke. These range from the major gap between Bath and Morgan's Hill to the 'gates' at various places where ancient trackways intersected with the dyke. In many places there are other significant gaps much too long to be gates. These mainly occur on West Wansdyke. The West Wansdyke Project has shown that in many locations where the bank is no longer visible it once existed but has since been ploughed out. However, there remain gaps where a combination of Colt Hoare's two hundred year old observations, aerial photographs, field walking and the West Wansdyke project's investigations has found no evidence of the earthwork. These are the one mile long Publow Hill gap, a smaller gap at Pennsylvania Farm and east of Englishcombe to the Breach Wood Valley for a distance of about two thirds of a mile. The Foxes also concluded that the dyke may be absent from the steep sided combe at the head of Padley Bottom close to where the dyke cuts the Fosse Way (Fox & Fox 1960 pp 35 and 37). The explanations for these gaps include the possibility that they were wooded areas at the time of the dyke's construction, that because of this a wooden palisade, which has since disappeared, was used as a barrier or that these stretches were considered of low priority and the builders simply never got round to them, perhaps because of a shortage of labour. Gaps on East Wansdyke occur around Old Shaw House and east of the A345 around Wernham Farm. Here the explanation seems to be that the bank did once exist but was destroyed by building works associated with Shaw House and the railway line from Marlborough respectively, or it was simply ploughed out.

Construction

Fowler and Erskine have given us a good idea of the method of construction, which was noted in the previous chapter. They have, bravely, attempted to estimate the resources required to construct the earthwork. Their conclusions are somewhat at variance from each other, but their estimates indicate that, depending on the size of the labour force available, which we have no means of knowing, the entire earthwork may well have been completed in weeks, or at most a few months, rather than years. It may reasonably be assumed that, for a project of this scale, the individual who had ordered it to be constructed would have had access to a substantial labour force, and would have needed co-operation from, and presumably authority over, communities or estate owners all along its length.

Purpose

That Wansdyke was a boundary marker almost goes without saying. Whether it was a defensive structure or not it was clearly meant to differentiate between one side and the other, if for no other purpose than to control movement. The Foxes proposed that it was built for defensive purposes on the chalk and as a territorial boundary elsewhere. However, even off the chalk the scale of the earthwork is such as to call into doubt whether it was conceived as nothing more than a boundary marker. It was a substantial construction which seems intended to act as an obstacle to movement, whereas a boundary could be marked by stones or a much lesser bank. It seems inconceivable that this level of resources was expended on something that was not envisaged as a defensive line.

The evidence is not forthcoming to support a manned, patrolled structure like Hadrian's Wall. There is no evidence of a patrol track or a palisade on the crest of the bank (Fox & Fox 1960 p 25), and there is no evidence of quarters for the troops manning the dyke other than the hillforts on West Wansdyke (Erskine 2007 p101). However, the Foxes note that there are various vantage points from which large sections of the dyke can be viewed. Most of West Wansdyke could be viewed from Stantonbury, and large sections from Maes Knoll or the high ground traversed by the Fosse Way south of Bath. From Tan Hill the whole of East Wansdyke from Morgan's Hill to West Woods can be seen, and arguably no enemy was going to attack through the wooded section to the east. Perhaps there was a degree to which it was assumed that the dyke was sufficient of a barrier not to need constant monitoring. Certainly, it would form a significant obstacle to horses, carts or livestock.

The British monk, Gildas, writing in the sixth century, was dismissive of the value of such an obstacle. In *De Excidio* he refers to a wall made of turf in the following terms:

> The British were told to construct across the island a wall linking the two seas; properly manned, this would scare away the enemy and act

as protection for the people. But it was the work of a leaderless and irrational mob, and made of turf rather than stone; so it did no good. (Gildas 15).

However, we do have at least one account of an earthwork playing a role in battle. In his Annals Book 2, Tacitus is relating the details of a campaign in northern Germany by Germanicus Caesar against the Angrivarii of Arminius in AD16. This was in reprisal for the heavy defeat the Angrivarii had inflicted on the Romans in the Teutoburg Forest in AD9. Here, Tacitus tells us that '. . . the Angrivarii had raised a broad earthwork, as a boundary between themselves and the Cherusci. Here their infantry was ranged. . .'. Germanicus had drawn up his infantry so that some would advance on level ground and some would clamber up the earthwork which confronted them. But we are told that:

> Those who had to assault the earthwork encountered heavy blows from above, as if they were scaling a wall. The general saw how unequal this close fighting was, and having withdrawn his legions to a little distance, ordered the slingers and artillerymen to discharge a volley of missiles and scatter the enemy (Tacitus Annals 2:24-25).

What this account tells us is that the earth bank was at least partially successful in resisting the enemy, and might have been wholly successful against a lesser force than the might of the Roman legions. Here, therefore we see an earth bank being used as both a boundary and for defence, and well before the earliest date that Wansdyke could have been built.

It seems plausible that such a defensive function did not require to be permanently patrolled providing there was sufficient advance warning of an enemy's approach. It could provide an obstacle which would slow down an advancing force and a good vantage point against which to defend against them. However, intelligence would be important, and the vantage points which we have already discussed may have had a function both as lookouts and as beacons from which to raise the alarm. Consequently, a defensive function for the earthwork can be supported.

It is also clear that another important purpose was to control traffic using the main north south routes across the area. We have seen that the dyke cuts a whole series of important routes, including the Jurassic Way, the Fosse Way, the London to Bath Roman Road and the Ridgeway. On the Ridgeway and in West Woods we have noted the construction of a series of gates which seem designed to channel and control movement. By contrast, the works at Morgan's Hill seem designed to take the Roman road out of action. At other places, most notably the crossing of the Fosse Way south of Bath, modern construction has obliterated any evidence there might have been for gates. Nonetheless, there are examples of gates, which allow us to draw a parallel with Hadrian's Wall. Fowler reminds us that Hadrian's Wall was much more than a means of separating the Romans from the barbarians. It was there to control movement, commercial as well as military, into and from the province. Such lines could have been built primarily for defence, or be statements about power and image and perception of a legitimate frontier (Fowler 2001 p 195). Perhaps if goods were in short supply in the post-Roman period it was necessary, or at least desirable, to try to control their movement, and maybe, in the process, to charge tolls on the carriers. In the Saxon period control of trade was important. The law code of King Ine of Wessex shows that he was particularly interested in controlling the activities of traders. Later, the laws of Alfred required traders to bring before a king's reeve at a public meeting the men whom they wished to take with them into the country (Yorke 1995 p299-300). A frontier line such as Wansdyke could easily be pressed into service for the purpose of controlling trade even if that was not what it was originally constructed for. By Saxon times we would be talking about a frontier between two kingdoms.

All these purposes are interlinked and suggest a need to control and maybe, if required, to resist movement to and from the north. In doing so, Wansdyke was part of a tradition of linear earthworks located in many parts of the country, a tradition which was already well established by Roman times.

Other Linear Structures

Wansdyke is by no means unique as a linear earthwork feature. It is part of a long tradition, both from Britain and abroad, which started well before it was built and continued through the Roman period into the Anglo-Saxon age.

Grim's Ditch is the name for a series of earthworks across the chalk in southern England. These earthworks, which are not related to each other, are located in Hampshire/Dorset, Wiltshire, Oxfordshire, Buckinghamshire, Berkshire and Harrow on the edge of London. They are generally agreed to date from the first millennium BC, and are named after Woden, for whom 'Grim' is another name. The two sections of Grim's Ditch closest to Wansdyke are the one associated with Bokerly Dyke on the border between Hampshire and Dorset where they meet Wiltshire, and a second running along Grovely Ridge in South Wiltshire on the south side of the Wylye Valley.

The section of Grim's Ditch associated with Bokerly Dyke is a straight section lying just to the south west of the latter. It is 1.7 metres from the bottom of the ditch to the top of the bank and a maximum of about 0.8 metres above ground level. Its date is unknown but is thought to be late Bronze Age or Early Iron Age, around 1000 to 500 BC. The section of Grim's Ditch on Grovely Ridge was studied by Desmond Bonney as part of his examination of early boundaries in Wessex. Here, the line of the ditch is followed very closely by a Roman Road. The ditch appears to be filled in where it is intersected by the road, indicating that it predates the Roman road. Certainly, the ditch was a boundary, perhaps a ranch boundary, from early times and still functions as such today. The dimensions of Grim's Ditch suggest that it was not built primarily with defence in mind but was mainly a boundary marker. Bokerly Dyke itself is considered to have its origins in the Bronze Age or Early Iron Age, though sections of it were much modified in Roman times, as shown by Pitt Rivers' excavations which we examined in the previous chapter.

The Romans are among the most famous builders of linear defences in history, and not just in Britain. In the second century AD they threw up a number of linear defences around many of their frontiers, known as *limes*. Hadrian's Wall and the Antonine Wall are part of this process, being constructed in 122 and 142 respectively. Other examples are in Germany, Romania, Arabia and North Africa. These took a variety of forms, as the two British examples demonstrate, Hadrian's Wall being a fully formed stone structure along much of its length while the Antonine Wall is an earth bank and ditch. It is often, though not always, the case that these frontiers made use of rivers instead of a built structure, where these were deemed to constitute a sufficiently robust boundary. This led the Foxes to comment that the use of rivers as defensive lines, in the case of Wansdyke the River Avon, would be consistent with the Roman tradition (Fox & Fox1960 p2).

Erskine characterised Wansdyke as a 'late Roman *limes* of the late fourth century'. He noted that it did not represent any technology not used by the Roman Empire. He showed that its measurements, form and constructional details corresponded closely to those given in Vegetius's *Epitoma Rei Militaris,* a manual for building simple marching camp defences used by Roman armies on the move. The *Epitoma*, dating from the late fourth century, describes a bank and ditch construction using turf blocks to start the process, and then timber revetments to support the earth bank during construction. The whole would normally be topped off by a palisade. The dimensions vary to suit the circumstances, but are not dissimilar to those of Wansdyke (Erskine 2008 pp 101-102).

Antonine Wall near Falkirk

A comparison between Wansdyke, the western third of Hadrian's Wall (which was initially a turf construction) and the Antonine Wall shows broadly similar dimensions. The northern walls tend to have larger ditches, that for the Antonine Wall being a mighty 12 metres wide and 3.5 metres deep, while that for Hadrian's Wall is 8.2 metres wide by 2.8 metres deep. The design of the turf bank on the northern walls is somewhat different also, it being a more upright, narrower structure than the bank at Wansdyke, which is more rounded. This bank is normally set back from the ditch by a berm, a 'shelf' of flat land, typically about 6 metres wide, within which obstacles might be placed, though this berm is not always present. These walls would have been constructed by organised legions rather than local work levies or the militia that might have constructed Wansdyke. And, of course, Wansdyke was built at least 200 years later, maybe much more (*ibid* p 103).

Two other dykes which may date from the Roman or post-Roman period are Bokerly Dyke (north of the Epaulment, demonstrated to be Roman by Pitt Rivers) and Wat's Dyke, which lies parallel to and a few miles east of the northern end of Offa's Dyke in North Wales. This section of Bokerly Dyke has a bank rising about 2.1 metres above ground level with a width of nearly 11 metres and a ditch 5.8 metres in width and originally about 3.7 metres deep (from Pitt Rivers Sections). As we saw in the last chapter, the Rear Dyke at Bokerly was Roman, but Pitt Rivers' believed that the Fore Dyke could have been built after the Romans had departed as it blocked the Roman road. Wat's Dyke's bank averages about 10 metres in width and 4 metres high from the bottom of the ditch, which is about 2 metres deep and 5 metres wide. The dating of Wat's Dyke is controversial, with the traditional view being that it was constructed in the early 8th century shortly before Offa's Dyke. However, this was challenged by the discovery of a hearth on the line of the Dyke which had been used just before it was buried. Radiocarbon dating puts the likely date range for the charcoal retrieved from the hearth to 411 to 561, right in the post-Roman period. However, as there is no evidence to link the construction of the hearth to the construction of the dyke this does not take us much further forward. Optically Stimulated Luminescence dating on Wat's Dyke indicates a much later ninth century date (Bell 2012 p74-5).

The construction of linear earthworks continued well beyond the post-Roman period, and the technique was adopted by the Anglo-Saxons. Of particular note are Offa's Dyke, the longest of the dykes, and

Devil's Dyke near Newmarket

the ditch systems of Cambridgeshire, most notably Devil's Dyke. Offa's Dyke is thought to date from the late 8th century on the assumption that it was built by Offa, as claimed by Asser, and the bank stands up to 2.5metres high. Devil's Dyke is up to a massive 10.5 metres from the bottom of its ditch to the top of its bank, and is thought to date from the 5th or 6th century (Devil's Dyke Restoration Project). In terms of the precedents established by other linear earthworks, we can say that although the technology existed for Wansdyke to have been built in the late Roman or post-Roman period, other, similar earthworks exist which are much later than this, and do not rule out Wansdyke being the 'Offa's Dyke of Wessex' as has been suggested (Reynolds 1999 p85).

This review of some of the major ditches is to demonstrate that Wansdyke is not an isolated example of a linear earthwork. There are a number of other examples which act as precedents for the design, construction and uses of Wansdyke, dating from possibly the end of the Bronze Age, through the Roman period into the Anglo-Saxon period. In other words, this was an established means of marking out boundaries and defending and controlling territory. A comprehensive review of these dykes has been undertaken by Mark Bell (Bell 2012)

Dating Evidence

We have already noted that the dating evidence for Wansdyke is very sparse, especially considering the extent of the earthwork. We have also noticed that the dyke is not particularly associated with the two types of site which are most helpful to archaeologists - settlements and cemeteries. No coins and little material that can be dated using radiocarbon dating or other techniques have been found. Dating from finds must therefore be somewhat tentative.

Finds

There are three sources of finds which can be used as dating evidence. These are the excavations by Pitt Rivers in the 1880s and 1890s, Stephen Green in the 1960s and The West Wansdyke Project in the 1990s.

It is still Pitt Rivers' finds which are the most convincing, but even he, by his own admission did not find a huge amount of dating evidence. To recap, the principal pieces of evidence were Samian Ware, which he was able to date to before the end of the third century, a knife and nails which he believed to be Roman and an iron cleat similar to those he had found at the cemetery at Bokerly Dyke associated with Roman coins. No coins were found at Wansdyke. This was sufficient for him to conclude that the earthwork was constructed in or after the Roman period.

The two subsequent excavations I have examined have not added greatly to these conclusions, though they have not contradicted them. Green found Samian Ware and Savernake or Broomsgrove pottery datable to the first century AD at Red Shore, together with other pottery which was more tentatively dated as Roman. He also found a pennanular brooch datable from the Iron Age onwards (Green 1971 p136).

Pitt Rivers' Nail and Cleat Display in Salisbury Museum (with kind permission of Salisbury Museum ©)

I have noted the summary of finds from the West Wansdyke Project in the

previous chapter. These consist of struck flints probably from the early
to middle neolithic period, and of a relatively small number of pottery
finds described as 'generic prehistoric' and Romano-British (Erskine
2008 p94). The Romano-British pottery is sufficient to endorse the
Roman *terminus post quem* for the dyke but the earlier finds, together
with the stratified nature of the bank, hint at a much earlier phase of
construction which was added to by the builders of Wansdyke.

This is not a lot to go on, and these finds only fix the earliest date
for construction. There are no later finds datable to the Anglo-Saxon
period.

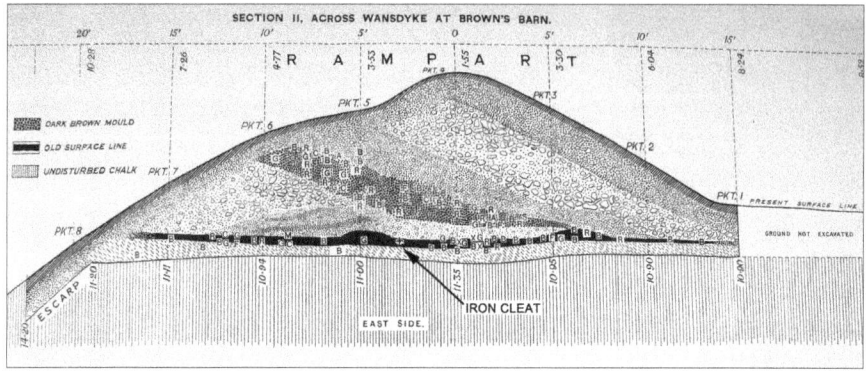

Pitt Rivers' Section at Brown's Barn

Radio Carbon Dating
Radio carbon dating is one of the archaeologist's most valuable tools
in dating an excavation. It has been attempted on Wansdyke, but with
little success. It was used by the West Wansdyke project in 1996
and at an excavation by the Trust for Wessex Archaeology (as Wessex
Archaeology was then known) at Wernham Farm, near New Buildings,
in 1985. Radiocarbon dating works on organic material, and is possible
if appropriate deposits, usually of charcoal or bone, can be uncovered.
However, the two radiocarbon examinations that have taken place on
samples from Wansdyke have given results that are both wildly different
from each other and from what might be expected from other evidence.

Radiocarbon dates were obtained from woody oak charcoal found
at Blackrock Lane as part of the West Wansdyke excavations. These gave
calibrated dates of between 1000BC and 520BC at 95% confidence, and

are therefore interpreted as belonging to an earlier, buried soil horizon (Erskine 2007 p92). Wessex Archaeology's investigations were carried out prior to the laying of the Esso Midline Oil Pipeline, which cut across the line of Wansdyke at Wernham Farm. A considerable amount of charcoal was obtained from near the bottom of the fill of the ditch which produced a date quoted as 1000, though Reynolds and Langlands later revealed that this was from a range of cal. 890-1160. The excavators knew that this date range ruled out a link with the construction of the earthwork, but argued that it securely dated a significant later event, which indicated that the bank had lost its defensive function by that time and may have been used as a dump for stone (Smith and Cox 1986 pp 20-21, Reynolds and Langlands 2006 p25)

This illustrates the difficulty of using radiocarbon dating to date the construction of the dyke as finds can emerge from contexts that have nothing to do with the time of construction. The two dates that have been obtained do not take us much further forward in identifying when the earthwork was built.

Charters and Other Written Sources
When it comes to a possible end date, the *terminus ante quem*, there is no archaeology to help us. The evidence comes from interrogating land charters from the period. The Stanton St Bernard Charter of 903 is the earliest to mention Wansdyke by name and is generally accepted as authentic (Electronic Sawyer S368). This is as good a source as could be wanted to set an end date for the window within which the earthwork could have been constructed. An earlier charter from Alton Priors, dating from 825, refers to *'thaere Ealden Dic'* (The Old Dyke), which has been taken as a reference to Wansdyke as it crossed the area in question. This charter is generally believed to be a much later forgery, but one which probably drew on contemporary sources (Grundy 1919 and Electronic Sawyer S272).

It has been traditionally held that because 'Wansdyke' is a pagan name it must have been constructed before the date of the conversion of the people of Wessex to Christianity. This is datable from Bede's *Historia Ecclesiastica* to 635, the date when Birinus baptised Cynegils, the king of Wessex. This date had often been accepted by scholars as the latest date at which Wansdyke could have been built, but it is hardly

irrefutable proof. The Foxes and Peter Fowler had different takes on how
to interpret the use of the name 'Wansdyke'. For Fowler it was a case of
its namers clearly having no idea who had built it and therefore calling
it in effect 'God's Dyke' (Fowler 2001 p195), but for the Foxes, it was
'improbable to say the least that such a sacred name should be given by
Saxons to any obsolete defence of their British enemy' (Fox & Fox 1960
p 40).

More recently, Draper and Reynolds and Langlands have
challenged this view. They argue that it was perfectly possible for the Dyke
to have been built after 635 for the following reasons. First, Christianity
was slow to take hold and vestiges of paganism would have clung on.
Second, Asser lists Woden among the ancestors of King Alfred:

> His genealogy is woven in this way. King Alfred was the son of King
> Aethelwulf, the son of Egbert the son of Ealhmund, the son of Eafa, the
> son of Eoppa, the son of Ingild . . . They [*Ingild and his brother King Ina*]
> were the sons of Cenred, the son of Ceolwold, the son of Cutha, the son
> of Cuthwine, the son of Ceawlin, the son of Cynric, the son of Creoda, the
> son of Cerdic, the son of Elesa, the son of Gewis (after whom the Welsh
> call the whole race the Gewisse), the son of Brand, the son of Baeldaeg,
> the son of Woden, the son of Frithuwald, the son of Frealaf, the son of
> Frithuwulf, the son of Finn, (the son of) Godwulf, the son of Geat (whom
> the pagans worshipped for a long time as a god) (Asser p67).

This was clearly not just acceptable but seen as adding to Alfred's
stature. It demonstrates that Woden and other pagans were 'live' figures
in Christian Anglo-Saxon England. Third, as we have seen above, clerics
continued to use the name in charters of the 10th century. The naming
of the dyke after Woden may express a desire to name the frontier
after a heroic figure with strong connections to the West Saxon royal
house. Parallels with Offa's Dyke are drawn with the inference that Offa
himself was named after a heroic ancestor of the same name (Reynolds
and Langlands 2006 pp 33-4, Draper 2006 p75).

This gives us a date range for construction of the earthwork
in its final form of around 350 to 903 at its widest. With this level of
uncertainty, scholars have also looked elsewhere for evidence on which
to date the dyke more closely.

Roman Road at Morgan's Hill

The Roman Road at Morgan's Hill

The junction between the Roman road and Wansdyke at Morgan's Hill is an important piece of dating evidence. In the 18th century William Stukeley believed that the Roman road cut through Wansdyke, and that the dyke therefore predated the Roman period. The Foxes took a more considered look with the benefit of two hundred years in the development of archaeological knowledge, and Pitt Rivers' dating evidence. They declared Stukeley to have been deceived. The track he thought cut through the counterscarp was modern and the Roman road was submerged under it. The counterscarp had cut across the road and the earthwork post-dated it. The Roman road is, in their words, 'effectively put out of action at this point' (Fox & Fox 1960 p5).

Elsewhere on the downs, Wansdyke cuts across other dykes and enclosures, as at the site of Pitt Rivers' excavations at Brown's Barn, but since the date of these other earthworks is not known this does not help us greatly.

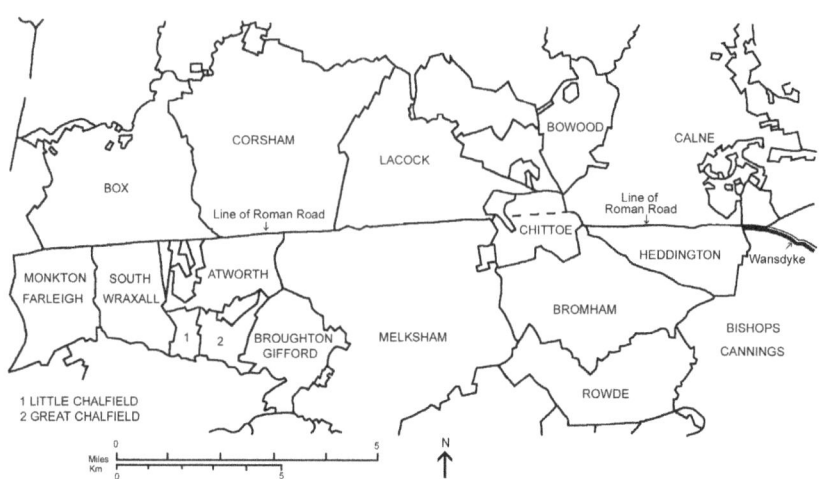

THE ROMAN ROAD AND PARISH BOUNDARIES BETWEEN EAST WANSDYKE AND BATH
(After Desmond Bonney)

Parish Boundaries in Relation to Roman Road, Bath to Morgan's Hill
(after Desmond Bonney)

Studies of Parish Boundaries

I have noted that Stephen Green quoted Desmond Bonney's examination
of parish boundaries in the discussion of his excavations at Red Shore.
At about the same time, Desmond Bonney had published the second
of two articles on the subject of ancient boundaries in Wessex, which
used Wansdyke as a case study. Bonney showed that parish boundaries
ignored Wansdyke and argued that they must therefore predate it.

This may seem rather arcane but it is an important issue for
Wansdyke. If Bonney was right then the date at which parish boundaries
or their predecessors were delineated in this area becomes important
evidence, particularly for those that argue for a later date for the dyke's
construction. Therefore I am going to explore this issue in a bit more
detail.

Bonney's thesis that parish boundaries are very old and have their
origins at least as early as the fifth century is demonstrated in the first
of his articles 'Pagan Saxon Burials and Boundaries in Wiltshire'. He
argues that while the ecclesiastical parishes, from which modern civil
parishes are derived, came into being in the 10th and 11th centuries,

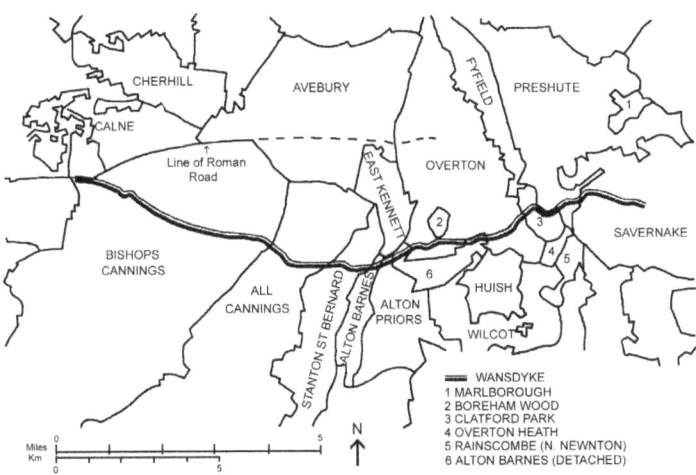

EAST WANSDYKE, THE ROMAN ROAD AND EARLY PARISH BOUNDARIES
(After Desmond Bonney)

Parish Boundaries in Relation to East Wansdyke
(after Desmond Bonney)

they have their origins in much older estate boundaries. This can be shown by comparing parish boundaries with the estate boundaries described in charters of the later Saxon period. He then examined the location of pagan Saxon burials of the fifth century and discovered that a disproportionate number of them lay on or very close to these ancient boundaries. From this he concluded that these boundaries go back at least as far as pagan Saxon times, ie before 635 (Bonney 1966 pp 25-31).

The second article is a chapter entitled 'Early Boundaries in Wessex' in *Archaeology in the Landscape* edited by Peter Fowler and published in 1972. In this article he shows very persuasively that the Roman road between Morgan's Hill and Bath forms parish boundaries along almost its entire length. Bonney went back to the boundaries shown in tithe maps of the 1840s to avoid any effect of modern realignments (Bonney 1972 p176), but in this particular instance we know that the Roman road still formed the local government boundary between West Wiltshire and North Wiltshire Districts, and therefore the parishes within them, until 2009.

Bonney then showed that East Wansdyke did not follow parish boundaries at all (a section of the dyke in West Woods became the parish boundary of Fyfield when the boundaries were redrawn in 1896 but that is not relevant to this analysis (Fowler 2001 p186)). The same is true of West Wansdyke, except, interestingly, the straight stretch at Combe Down, which could well follow a Roman road. His conclusion is that, in this area, parish boundaries were established in Roman times. The fact that they ignore Wansdyke is further evidence that Wansdyke was built after the Roman road.

Bonney showed that in south Wiltshire, on Grovely Ridge, parish boundaries followed the older Grim's Ditch rather than the Roman road from Charterhouse to Old Sarum which follows the earthwork quite closely. His explanation for this was that the boundaries probably go back to Iron Age times. Where there was evidence of settlement in Iron Age times, as on Grovely Ridge, older boundaries were followed. He argued that the area through which the Roman road from Morgan's Hill to Bath passed was not heavily occupied in Iron Age times. The Roman road opened it up. Estates were marked out on either side of the road, probably for the first time, and it is these boundaries that have endured (*ibid* pp 178 and 181).

Why do parish boundaries ignore a major feature such as the dyke, which was, after all, intended to be a boundary marker? Sometimes the extent to which parish boundaries ignore Wansdyke is by quite minor amounts, leaving small areas of parish seemingly on the 'wrong' side of Wansdyke (*ibid* p 176). This is contrasted with Bokerly Dyke, which became an important boundary, and remains so to this day (*ibid* p 183). This is seen as evidence of the ephemeral nature of Wansdyke. Had it remained a significant feature for a long period it would surely have become an administrative boundary in due course.

For Reynolds and Langlands and Draper the dates at which these boundaries came into being is an important part of their argument for a later, 7th or 8th century, date for the construction of Wansdyke. Both accept Bonney's premise that Wansdyke post dates the definition of parish, or estate boundaries, but both claim that parish boundaries were defined much later than Roman times, and Wansdyke could therefore not have been built as early as this. They cite Dr. Della Hooke's extensive work on boundaries and other evidence which suggest that they were defined between the ninth and the twelfth centuries. The evidence is derived largely from the number of charters granting small parcels of land dating from the middle of the tenth century compared with far fewer grants of earlier or later dates. The emergence of enclosed 'thegnly' residences with a hall and associated church and settlement at about the same time is seen as adding weight to this scenario (Reynolds and Langlands 2006 pp26-31).

Della Hooke has studied the development of parish boundaries in great detail. She was of the view that although individual estates became more or less stable units in the 9th, 10th and 11th centuries, subdivision may have started in Pagan Saxon times, largely the same argument as Desmond Bonney (Hooke 1998 p68).

Andrew Reynolds has examined the evidence provided by execution cemeteries. These are consistently located on significant territorial boundaries. A series of execution sites which can be scientifically dated to the seventh and eighth centuries indicate an earlier recognition of territorial limits, at least at the level of the hundred, outside the Danelaw (Reynolds 2011 p901). This is a similar argument to Bonney's in relation to burials on boundaries, though he comes to a later conclusion on dates.

We can probably not reach a final conclusion on this. Della Hooke has described this debate as largely fruitless 'for as one moves back in time so the evidence becomes flimsy or non-existant, leaving too much room for speculation' (Hooke 1998 p63).

Although Bonney's argument makes sense, estate boundaries may actually have nothing to do with this issue. These estates were functional units, designed to a large extent to be self-sufficient. The objective was for them to contain a mixture of pasture, arable and meadow, and if they did not already possess sufficient of any one of these attempts were made to secure it, sometimes in areas detached from the main estate. Thus, whether or not a boundary followed a feature such as a road might be totally irrelevant. In the Wylye Valley the Roman road is ignored and in the Vale of White Horse the Ridgeway is ignored (Hooke 1998 p81). By the same token Wansdyke may well have been ignored if it was not helpful to the assemblage of the necessary land. On the Marlborough Downs there are a number of earlier dykes, some of which were cut by Wansdyke, and others may have contributed to its earlier phases, but these have also been ignored by parish boundaries.

In fact, we can see that in most cases where Wansdyke does not follow a parish boundary, it is nowhere near that boundary, in some cases running right through the middle of the parish. In other cases, such as at Combe Down, south of Bath and in West Woods, it actually follows the parish boundary for short distances, presumably because it was helpful to do so. The examples which have caused the greatest difficulty are those where the parish boundary is 'clipped' with tiny areas the 'wrong' side of the earthwork. These really only occur at Alton Barnes and Alton Priors, and to a lesser extent at Stanton St Bernard, all typical long, thin, downland parishes descending from the top of the Marlborough Downs to the Vale of Pewsey to achieve the mix of land uses. At Alton Priors we know from the 825 charter that the relevant land north of Wansdyke was described as a 'gore' or ploughland in common occupation, which may in fact have been delineated by the dyke (Grundy 1919 pp159-164). It may have been 'left-over' land but, rather than give it up to another parish, it was given a specific use. At Stanton St Bernard the area north of the dyke was marked by several boundary stones whose antiquity we do not know (*ibid* pp 210-215).

While this issue adds weight to the later scenario for the construction of Wansdyke, it is by no means as straight forward as Bonney originally made it appear, and it doesn't necessarily rule out earlier scenarios.

Hillforts

We have noted that West Wansdyke incorporates at least two hillforts into its structure: Maes Knoll and Stantonbury. Others may be included if the additional sections of earthwork are taken into account; Stokeleigh Camp and Bathampton. East Wansdyke has no hillforts on its line, though it passes close to the hillfort of Rybury. If the postulated eastern extension is taken into account then Chisbury is also on the line.

The incorporation of hillforts into the dyke is seen by some commentators as evidence that the structure is Romano-British rather than Anglo-Saxon (Yorke 1995 p22, Dark 2001). For instance, Barbara Yorke specifically comments:

> West Wansdyke appears from its relationship with Roman features to be post-Roman, and the most likely contexts for it are either the period of refortification of hillforts in the late fifth and sixth centuries or the competition between Wessex and Mercia in the seventh and eighth

centuries. The balance is tipped in favour of the earlier date by the inclusion of two hillforts within the line of the dyke . . . (Yorke 1995 p22)

We will discuss this comment in relation to the earlier date below, but the initial point to note is the preference for the post-Roman rather than mid-Anglo-Saxon date. The proposition is that the reoccupation of hillforts was a distinctly British phenomenon, and, further, that there was no tradition of the use of hillforts in the homelands of the Germanic incomers (Dark 2000 p142). Even the British had ceased to use hillforts in the areas they still controlled by about 700, so it is unlikely that they would have been in use at the end of the 8th century. They were pressed into service again as *burhs* to defend against the Viking invasions by Alfred in the second half of the ninth century. Chisbury, for example, was one of the *burhs* listed in the *Burghal Hidage*. But this is later, and in different circumstances to the scenario proposed by Reynolds and Langlands. Dark suggests that Offa's Dyke may have incorporated hillforts, citing the example of Old Oswestry (Dark 1994 p224). If this were the case it could be evidence from the late eighth century. However, Old Oswestry lies on Wat's Dyke but is some two miles from the line of Offa's dyke.

The inclusion of Maes Knoll and Stantonbury is usually held to be evidence linking construction of the dyke to the Durotriges in the late fifth or sixth century. There are difficulties with this interpretation which I have already pointed out. It works for West Wansdyke but is unsatisfactory for East Wansdyke. Laycock has argued that reoccupation of hillforts may have been earlier than previously supposed on the basis of belt buckles from the fourth century found in hillforts at Stanwick, Yorkshire, Penycorddyn in North Wales and Blewburton in Berkshire. This supports his case for tribal disputes at the end of the Roman period, which, in turn, could provide a context for the construction of Wansdyke (Laycock 2008 p156).

Worm Working
Bruce Eagles and Michael Allen draw our attention to another controversial issue, which, with so little other dating evidence, may be relevant. They quote a letter they received from Tony Clark, which argues, on the basis of observations by Charles Darwin on worm action,

that it is possible to estimate the date of deposition of a find by its depth in relation to the original ground surface on it was deposited. Burial by worms takes place at an average rate of 4cm in ten years. Tony Clark's analysis of Pitt Rivers' sections at Brown's Barn was that the distribution of pottery within and beneath the bank showed that there was very little time for worm action to take place between the cessation of deposition and the building of the dyke, in his opinion no more than forty years. The authors do not endorse these precise conclusions but do suggest that, when taken with the fact that the sherds illustrated by Pitt Rivers seem to have relatively fresh edges and be largely unworn, it could support an early date for construction, though the evidence is not robust enough to be certain (Eagles 2018 Chapter 5).

Coin Hoards
East Wansdyke is notable for the important coin hoards that have been found close by. These coin hoards are to be found on the southern side and are of late Roman date, so they fall within the time horizon which other evidence points to as one of the possible construction dates for the dyke. Here, we are very much in the realms of circumstantial evidence. However, the connections between the coin hoards and the earthwork deserve to be explored if for no other reason than to provide context for the times in which the dyke could have been built. Keith Nurse examined the connection in some detail in his 2002 paper 'Late Roman Coin Hoards and Wansdyke' (Nurse 2002). He highlights two coin hoards at Stanchester and Bishops Cannings which were found very close to Wansdyke and contain coins from the early fifth century.

The Stanchester hoard was found by a local schoolboy at Wilcot, near Pewsey, in 2000. It was close to an important villa site, Stanchester, after which it is named. This is only about 2 miles south of Wansdyke, where it passes through West Woods. The find contained 1196 coins in a grey flagon of Alice Holt ware. The latest coins in the group were dated to 406, making them the latest Roman coins to be found in Wiltshire. Nurse points to the work of Margaret Gelling, who argued that the suffix '-chester' attached to the name of villas by the Saxons denoted sites of particular importance. On this basis Nurse makes the case that late Roman villas had become administrative centres including among their functions the collection of taxes.

The Bishops Cannings Hoard was discovered in 1992 about a mile from Morgan's Hill. It contained over 7400 coins, the majority being bronze, an appreciable number silver and one gold. It is particularly important for its Valentinianic coins, dating from 364-378, but, importantly, the latest coins date from 395-402. Unlike the Stanchester Hoard, this contained clipped silver siliquae, and is considered to be the most important of this type in the West Country. The practice of clipping was to extract metal, probably for the purpose of counterfeiting. It is almost exclusively found in Britain and in coins dating from the reign of Honorius (393-423). It is argued that they are an indication of post-Roman practice as they are almost exclusively found in hoards buried after the end of the fourth century and with coins of the period of Honorius. The hoard also included bronze bowls, a military belt fitting and jewellery.

Further Valentinianic coins have been found at All Cannings. At Wayside Farm on the edge of Devizes coins from the period 388-402 have been found. In 2005, a hoard of 3854 silver and copper alloy coins was found at Alton Barnes, though these coins are a little earlier than the ones described above, being from the late third century. Many of these coins are on display at the Wiltshire Museum in Devizes.

Nurse then considers the significance of *Cunetio*, where the largest Roman coin hoard of all, consisting of 55,000 coins, had been discovered in 1978. As we have already seen, *Cunetio* is very close to Wansdyke. Its military importance is clear, and Nurse points to it also functioning as a tax collecting administrative centre (Nurse 2002). Moorhead has shown that sites in Wiltshire have a much larger proportion of Valentinianic coins than the national average. Moreover, this seems to apply particularly to sites in the north of the County. He observes that ' when sites in northern Wiltshire were generally flourishing in the second half of the 4th century, it looks as if others in the south were not, and this south Wiltshire decline is paralleled across the border in Dorset and Hampshire' (Moorhead 2001 pp96-7). This suggests that north Wiltshire was an area of particular interest to the Romans in the last years of empire. The above average levels of coinage could be due to military activity. Nurse links the high level of bronze coinage found in the area as evidence of this as it was used to finance the military at the time (Nurse 2002). The most obvious explanation is that it was the scene of unrest, and this could be linked to a spate of villa fires occurring at this time, which we will look at in the next chapter.

This would provide a possible context for the construction of Wansdyke, and also for the number of coin hoards. In a period of unrest coins are arguably safer in the ground than in someone's villa in days when there were no banks. Large sums of money could be being stored to pay for military activity or the construction of defences such as Wansdyke. The evidence of coin hoards does not demonstrate a direct link with the construction of Wansdyke, at least not at present. It does suggest periods of unrest in the vicinity, certainly in the late fourth century and possibly in the fifth century. A fifth century date may be implied by the amount of coin of early fifth century date being discovered in the area, which certainly suggests the resources to pay soldiers or to finance the construction of the dyke at this time.

The motives for burying coins are difficult to arrive at. It could represent a time of uncertainty, and this would be supported by the fact that the hoards were never reclaimed. On the other hand, it does not require a period of unrest in order to need a place of safety for valuables. Equally, it could be the case that people felt more secure burying coins after Wansdyke was constructed, and the fact that so many hoards have been found on its south side supports this view. Clearly, the argument can be made either way, and does not take us much further forward.

Conclusion

Archaeology has enabled us to answer many questions about Wansdyke. But we are still left with a wide date range, and a number of possibilities for when it could have been constructed, who by and why, because the period in question was one of huge changes which transformed the history of these Islands. This is an issue which bedevils the study of many of these earthworks for reasons that I have explained. In the absence of further archaeological studies, our only option to narrow things down further is to look at the wider context within which Wansdyke may have been built – what was going on in what we now call Somerset and Wiltshire between the end of the fourth century and the beginning of the tenth.

5
Historical Context

If the archaeology of Wansdyke cannot give us the whole story, then we need to turn to other sources to try to fill in the gaps. The approach will be to review the historical context over the period within which Wansdyke could have been constructed, ie about 350 to 903AD, drawing on archaeological evidence for locations other than Wansdyke and its immediate environs, focussing particularly on Somerset, Wiltshire and the adjoining areas. In doing this, I will draw heavily on Bruce Eagles' book *From Roman Civitas to Anglo-Saxon Shire: Topographical Studies on the Formation of Wessex*, which, as its title suggests, covers in detail exactly the time and place we are interested in. For each period we need to ask two questions. First, was Wansdyke a border between two polities at the time, and, second, was there a scenario for conflict between these polities?

Sub-divisions of Western Britain in Roman Times

Britain was not a single country before the Romans came. It was occupied by a number of tribes in the late Iron Age. Although Rome established the *Diocese of Britain*, which comprised England as far north as Hadrian's Wall and Wales for most of its life, it was subdivided into three further layers. First there were the provinces, initially two, subsequently four and reference made to a fifth, Valentia, that no-one has been able to locate geographically. The province of *Britannia Prima* occupied much of south west England, the west Midlands and Wales in terms of today's geography. Its chief town was Cirencester. Below this were the *civitates* (singular *civitas*), which are roughly equivalent to today's counties, though they were a little bigger, and these were subdivided into *pagi* about which little is known. It is at the level of the *civitas* that we can best start to examine the context for Wansdyke.

Our only knowledge of the locations of the *civitates* comes from Ptolemy's *Geographia*. This was a remarkable work of seven volumes produced in the middle of the second century AD, its author being a Roman citizen of Greek origin living in Egypt. It contains maps and a gazetteer of the Roman Empire. Chapter 2 of Book II covers mainland Britain; modern day England, Scotland and Wales. It contains descriptions of coastal landmarks and rivers and lists the tribes and their chief towns, giving a latitude and longitude for each location. When it comes to the tribes, he starts in the north and lists them all relative to each other moving south. This is all we have to go on. Ptolemy does not give us boundaries for the *civitates;* these can at best only be inferred from his lists.

On the basis of the *Geographia* we can deduce the following for the area we are interested in. In the north of the area, occupying modern day Gloucestershire and northern Wiltshire as well as areas further north, were the Dobuni or Dobunni, whose chief town was *Corinium,* or Cirencester. Next to them were the Atrebates, whose chief town was *Calleva Atrebatum,* or Silchester, between Reading and Basingstoke. They occupied modern day Berkshire and Northern Hampshire and probably the eastern side of Wiltshire. Below the Dobunni were the Belgae, not the pre-Roman tribe of Stukeley and Colt Hoare, but a Roman creation, whose origins we will examine in more detail later. Ptolemy lists three towns for them, *Iscalis, Aquae Calidae and Venta. Venta,* or *Venta Belgarum,* is Winchester, the civitas capital. *Aquae Calidae* is generally taken to be Bath, though this was more normally known as *Aquae Sulis* in Roman times. *Iscalis* is a bit of a puzzle. The latitude and longitude given by Ptolemy would place it on or near the coast of the Bristol Channel, while the *isca* prefix relates to water. Uphill, at the mouth of the River Axe south of Weston-super-Mare, fits the description well. Cheddar is another possibility, situated on the River Axe, which may have been tidal up to this point. The function of either of these ports would have been to serve the lead and silver mines on the Mendip Hills at Charterhouse, and Charterhouse itself is another candidate for *Iscalis* (Higgins 2005 pp 7-9, Leach 2001 p72, Eagles 2018 pp 7 & 8). Whichever of these locations it was it places the Mendip Hills in the *civitas Belgarum.* It can be seen from this that, according to Ptolemy, the *civitas* occupied a large crescent stretching from south Hampshire to north Somerset and incorporating much of central and southern Wiltshire. West and south of the Belgae are the Durotriges, whose chief town is named by

Ptolemy as *Dunium,* which is thought to be Hod Hill. In fact, Dorchester *(Durnovaria)* became the chief town of the Durotriges, who occupied central and south Somerset and Dorset. West of the Durotriges were the Dumnonii, whose chief towns were *Voliba,* whose location is unknown, *Uxella,* thought to be Launceston, *Tamara,* thought to be Plymouth, and *Isca,* which is Exeter. They occupied Cornwall, Devon and west Somerset.

Archaeologists have traditionally sought to define the *civitas* areas in more detail by reference to late Iron Age coin distributions. In the late Iron Age several British tribes used coinage from which we can tell much about who they were and what areas they occupied. This does seem to indicate that, for the most part, the Romans adopted Iron Age tribal areas for their *civitates.* However, Eagles cautions against reliance on this to establish detailed boundaries, arguing that the areas where such coinage is found have more to do with the ebb and flow of power and influence of individual rulers outside their own areas (Eagles 2018 p1).

Nonetheless, we can identify approximate areas for most of these Iron Age tribes, but not the Belgae. This *civitas* seems to have been based on the former territory of the Atrebates. There is a link here. On mainland Europe at that time was the Nation of the Belgae, who occupied what is now Belgium and eastern France down as far as about Switzerland. The Atrebates were a Belgic tribe who moved across the English Channel in Iron Age times to occupy central southern England. They issued coinage and we can approximately identify an area for them. These were the *Belgae* of Stukeley and Colt Hoare, predating the Romans. The choice of the name *Belgae* for the Roman *civitas* clearly implies a link.

This is all fairly straightforward and clear, and in many respects we should be grateful that we have this level of detail from the past. However, scholars have questioned some of Ptolemy's conclusions. A particular focus for this has been what is now north Somerset. It is argued that north Somerset is too detached from the *civitas* capital of Winchester and the only part which was not previously Atrebatic territory to be part of the civitas of the Belgae (eg Dark 2000 p148). However, Ptolemy mentions two places in north Somerset among his three towns of the Belgae (though Cunliffe regards the inclusion of Bath as a misidentification (Cunliffe 1993 p235)), and describes the Durotriges as being located west *and south* of the Belgae, not just west.

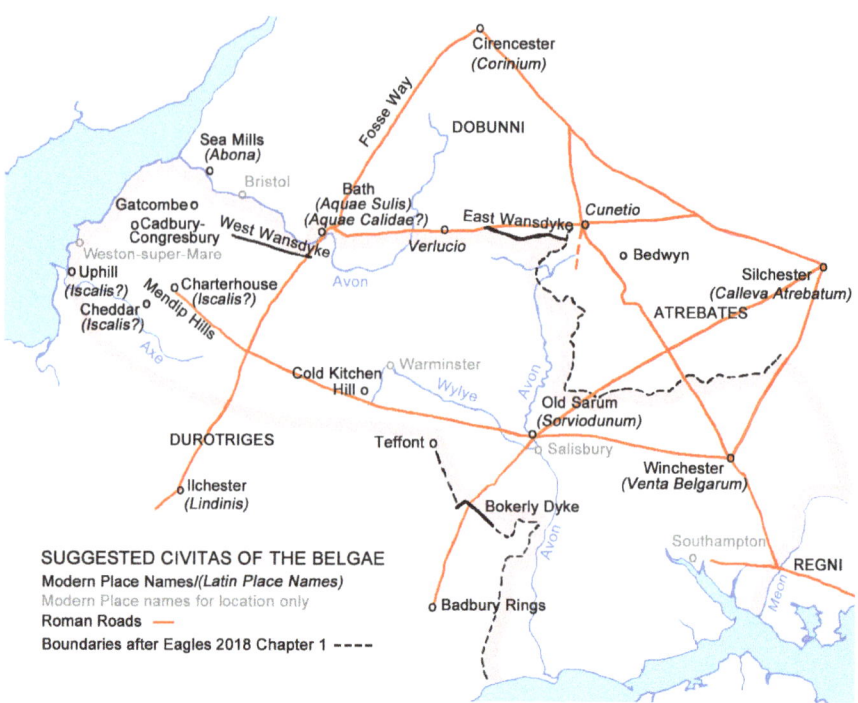

Suggested extent of the Civitas of the Belgae. Contains OS data © Crown copyright Open Data 1997.

He clearly thought that north Somerset was part of *civitas Belgarum*.

North Somerset is in an area where two of the major concentrations of Iron Age coinage overlap. Some commentators term these the 'western' and 'south western' distributions (Eagles 2018 p7), which have been linked to polities which became the *civitates* of the Dobunni and the Durotriges respectively in Roman times (Cunliffe 2005 chapters 7 and 8). There was no 'third' coinage distribution which might have corresponded to the Belgae. This has led some to the conclusion that *Civitas Belgarum* was a creation of the Romans, rather than the Romanisation of a pre-existing tribal area, and a case has been argued that it was a specially created Imperial canton designed to protect and control the region's significant mineral and agricultural resources which were located on the Mendip Hills (Higgins 2005 pp 17-18). It may well have amalgamated the territories of a number of small tribes, particularly in the west (Eagles 2018 p7). This would help to explain why it is such a large area which is seemingly not very homogeneous and also, perhaps, why the main Roman road out of the area leads south east directly towards Winchester, passing Old Sarum on the way (ref OS *Map of Roman Britain*, Costen 2011 p13).

Bruce Eagles has looked in detail at the possible boundaries of the *civitates* of this part of Britain. He has argued that the northern boundary of the *Belgae* followed the River Avon upstream as far as Bath, then the Roman Road from Bath to Silchester, then the line of East Wansdyke, on the assumption that its line is based on pre-existing, albeit intermittent, boundaries having their origin in prehistory. The eastern boundary of the *civitas* with the Atrebates may well have followed what became the boundary of the Kinwardstone Hundred in the area of Savernake Forest, as we have discussed in Chapter 2. This could explain the location of the eastern termination of East Wansdyke, as New Buildings is very close to this boundary. It turns out, therefore, that it is quite probable that Wansdyke could run on or close to the northern boundary of the *Belgae* (Eagles 2018 pp 1-8).

The End of Roman Britain

We have established a late Roman date as the earliest time when Wansdyke could have been built. This coincides with the period of decline in Roman Britain which ultimately ended in the departure of the Romans, traditionally dated to Honorius's *rescript* of 410AD in which he told the *civitates* to look to their own defences.

The archaeology of the late fourth century is plentiful and very visible. By contrast, the archaeology of the later fifth century is much less plentiful (Esmonde Cleary 2011 pp13-14). Of the most important archaeological indicators, production of both coinage and pottery ceased, building in stone made way for timber construction and burial evidence that can be dated to a sub-Roman British context is extremely scarce. Historical sources for the fifth century are thin on the ground and of doubtful reliability in many cases. Yet, the years after the formal Roman presence ceased are an important time in which, arguably, the foundations of our modern nations were laid. The paucity of the evidence for what actually happened has led to different models being proposed to shed light on this.

The notion of Britain as a 'failed state' has resonance, particularly in the light of modern day events in places such as the former Yugoslavia,

Afghanistan and other locations (cf Laycock 2008, Esmonde Cleary 2011). This characterises the change as rapid and chaotic. It postulates the emergence of competing tribes under the leadership of warlords as Roman law and order failed. Meanwhile, others seek to emphasise the continuity of life in Britain after the departure of the Romans, describing it as a society of 'late antiquity' whose inhabitants still regarded themselves as Roman well into the fifth century and possibly into the sixth (cf Dark 2000).

Esmonde Cleary argues that the two approaches are not fundamentally different. They shift the timing rather than the fundamental understanding of events (Esmonde Cleary 2011 p20). So it is perhaps not surprising that writers from both schools of thought find a place for Wansdyke in their models. Both Stuart Laycock and Ken Dark have examined the context for the construction of Wansdyke in some detail from these two different perspectives (Laycock 2008; Dark 2000). Both link the construction of the Dyke to inter-tribal conflict at some point in the fifth century, though Laycock's hypothesis would also allow a late fourth century date, on the basis that the collapse in law and order happened before the Romans had formally left, while Dark extends the possible construction period into the sixth century.

The area in which Wansdyke is situated is very much part of southern, lowland Britain, where Romanisation had been the most complete. In the early years of empire, it was accompanied by technological innovation and improvements which increased material wealth and was therefore enthusiastically embraced by the indigenous elite and new urban classes. The first problems began to appear in the third century when Rome failed to maintain economic, demographic and territorial expansion and this encouraged barbarian assaults and rebellions (Higham 1992 pp210-12).

In the fourth century taxation and bureaucracy increased to a level that was becoming unsustainable, as the province of Britannia became a diocese with four or five provinces. Under strain from decreasing revenue the size of the army was reduced with a consequent lack of security. Towns, which had flourished in the early years of the Empire, were now in decline as the elite moved to the countryside, with villas now becoming the focus for much economic activity. Crafts began a slow decline as markets dwindled (*ibid* pp 212-14).

In 367 there was a particularly serious incident, recorded by Ammianus, known as the Barbarian Conspiracy. Whether this was the only such incident we do not know, and many of the details of this event are skirted over. We are told that the Picts, Attacotti and Scots, all from modern day Scotland, began attacking and plundering various parts of Britain. Nectarides, the Count of the sea coast, had been killed and Duke Fullofaudes had been taken prisoner. The Roman general, Theodosius, set out for Britain with a large army and dealt with the insurgency. We learn that he invited deserters and others to join his army, indicative of the fact that the armed forces already stationed in Britain were in a poor state. Finally, we learn that Theodosius restored those cities and fortresses which had been damaged or destroyed (Laycock 2008 pp110-111).

Laycock notes that archaeologists have failed to find any evidence of the uprising, but then there may not have been much to find. Also, he casts doubt on whether the Picts, Scots and Attacotti would have reached as far south as London, which is the only location specifically linked to Theodosius's activities by Ammianus. He speculates that either tribes from the north of England, such as the Brigantes, had been part of the uprising, or that raiders from the southern civitates had joined in taking advantage of a crisis that originated in the north (*ibid* pp 112-3).

This may provide an explanation for *Cunetio* being refortified at this time. As we have seen, substantial refortification took place there, with a likely date after 360AD and it may well have become a regional administrative or military centre at this time (Corney 2001 p 18). Gatcombe, south west of Bristol, was an important settlement also fortified in the late fourth century with walls 5 metres thick (Leach 2001 p118, HER MNS593). This seems to be indicative of significant unrest in various places related to Wansdyke in the late fourth century.

There was other evidence of instability in the area. There is a particular concentration of villa fires at locations on or near the line of Wansdyke, which is worthy of note. Kings Weston Villa, on the western edge of Bristol, shows burning to its west wing datable to between 335 and 380. Brislington Villa, on the eastern edge of Bristol shows signs of burning and the bones of humans and cattle had been tipped into a well at some time between 337 and 370. At Keynsham Villa, a short distance to the east of Bristol, there is evidence of a fire datable to before 375.

There are then three sites in the vicinity of the Roman road east of Bath. At Box two rooms were burnt and the series of coins found on site ends with a coin of Valens (364-378). At Atworth, again two rooms were burnt, the incident being datable to around 340 to 375. At North Wraxall bones from three skeletons were dumped in a well, probably some time in the fourth century. Two sites south of Bath, Combe Down and Wellow, were also burnt, though the events cannot be dated. However, occupation at Combe Down seems to be fourth century ending in about 370. Finally, there is a group of villas around *Verlucio*. The villa at Bowood House produced evidence of burning and six skeletons. A villa at Calne with evidence of fourth century occupation produced more signs of fire and bones. A villa at West Park Field produced burnt bones and a coin series ending with Constantius II (324 - 361). At Nuthills Villa there were signs of attack and a coin series ending with Magentius (350 - 353) (Laycock 2008 p 140).

The plan shows the location of the villa fires. The proximity of their location both to each other and to the line of Wansdyke is striking. While there is no proof that the events occurred at more or less the same time, again the proximity of their dates is striking. The dates are also quite close to the 'Barbarian Conspiracy' of 367, and the refortification of *Cunetio*. A picture of unrest in this area around the time of the conspiracy looks compelling. It is also noticeable that the majority of the incidents were on the north side of the line of Wansdyke. If there is a connection with Wansdyke, there are two possible explanations for this. The first is aggression on the part of those living to the south of the line, at this time probably the Belgae, which failed. However, this fails to explain the fires south of the line. The second is aggression from the north. This aggression might have been successful, pushing the Belgae back, forcing the construction of a defensive barrier. This would explain why Bath, which was probably in *Civitas Belgarum* originally, was excluded from the territory defended.

Who would have been responsible for such aggression? Branigen quotes Irish raiders. This is dismissed by Laycock, who sees a likely link with Wansdyke (Laycock 2008 p141). The fact that *Cunetio* was refortified at this time strongly suggests that the Barbarian Conspiracy had reached this far south, and that it could be the cause of the fires. The other explanation is that the Dobunni, the civitas to the north of the Belgae, might have seized the opportunity created by the unrest to

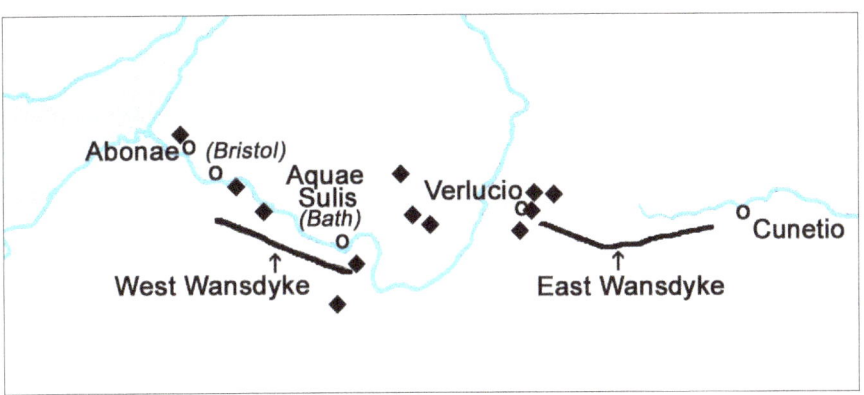

Location of Villa Fires in the vicinity of Wansdyke. Contains OS data © Crown copyright Open Data 2005.

regain old territory. I have been careful to relate the fire to 'the line of Wansdyke' in this section. The fires do not prove a link to Wansdyke, far from it. Draper dismisses the fires as having been caused accidentally on the basis of hearths and kilns which were found at the villas indicative of reuse for industrial processes (Draper 2006 p29). However, the number of fires in such a relatively confined area does provide a plausible scenario for unrest in the area in the late 4th century which could have led to the construction of Wansdyke.

Historical sources tell us that in the final years of the Roman presence in Britain there were a series of rebellions. The first was by Magnus Maximus in 383. According to the fifth century historian, Sozomen, writing in Constantinople, he set off for Rome with an army made up of Britons, Gauls, Celts and other nations. The rebellion was unsuccessful and Magnus Maximus met his death at Aquileia in northern Italy in 388 (Laycock 2009 p33). A second rebellion, led by Constantine III in 409 had its genesis in soldiers in Britain appointing a man known only as Marcus as their emperor. He was quickly replaced by Gratian, who in turn was replaced by Constantine III. Constantine, following in the footsteps of Magnus Maximus, led an army onto the continent heading for Rome in a bid to become emperor, although under the pretext of dealing with an invasion of the Vandals, Alans and Sueves who had crossed the frozen River Rhine in the winter of 406 (*ibid* pp24-8). Deserted by his General, Gerontius, he was eventually captured by the Romans and executed in 411.

During this time, the Britons back home felt that Constantine had left them undefended against Saxon raids and rebelled against him in 409, as did the Armoricans in present day Brittany. The rebels expelled the Roman administration and seceded from the Empire. This was effectively the end of Rome in Britain, and Emperor Honorius's *rescript*, telling the *civitates* to look to their own defences, may only have been a recognition of the inevitable (*ibid* p37 and Dark 2000 p 30).

Laycock argues that it is quite feasible that both Constantine's and Gerontius's forces included militiamen from British tribal militias as well as regular troops. Indeed, the presence of militias may have contributed to a new found confidence leading to two rebellions within 25 years (Laycock 2008 pp30-4). This is significant because for most of the period of Roman occupation civilians were unarmed. The British cleric Gildas refers to the fact that the Romans armed the Britons before they finally left Britain (*ibid* p23). Lacock proposes that there is evidence for the rearming of the local population of central, southern and eastern Britain in this period along tribal or *civitas* lines. The evidence for this is that from about 370 large numbers of military belt buckles begin to appear across Britain on both military and civilian sites. Many seem to have been manufactured here. Moreover, there is evidence of different designs associated with different *civitas* areas, including the Dobunni (Laycock 2008 pp 113-8). Certainly, the rebellion of 409 suggests that the British had some ability to defend themselves. Laycock dismisses the case that civilians in government service also wore belts on the grounds of the heavy concentration of buckles in military zones on the frontier of the Empire in continental Europe, and argues that civilians would not want to wear the cumbersome leather and metal belt set (*ibid* pp 114-6).

We therefore have clear evidence of unrest, which may have spread as far south as *Cunetio* and, by association, the surrounding area, which would have included the location of Wansdyke. We have also noted the incidence of villa fires in the area along the line of Wansdyke, probably at about this time. In addition, we have the possibility that, in the wake of the Barbarian Conspiracy, the Dobunni may have been rearming. Finds of late fourth century/early fifth century belt buckles extend into Wiltshire, that is Belgic territory, but are generally absent from Durotrigan and Dumnonic territory (*ibid* p 115).

The timing of these events is a little unclear. Laycock advances more evidence for disruption in the last quarter of the fourth century. Besides the villa fires, there is an unusually high incidence of unretrieved coin hoards in the south west of the Country. The biggest group of these are in modern day Somerset and Wiltshire, south of the line of Wansdyke, which we have already discussed, but another significant group lies on the boundary between the Dobunni and their eastern neighbours, the Catuvellauni (*ibid* pp 97 and 138). We have already noted that hoarding went on into the fifth century. Evidence of the decline of the pottery industry ties in with this. In the area south of Wansdyke, the New Forest Pottery industry was flourishing in the early fourth century. However, it was in decline in the second half of the fourth century and may have ceased production as early as 370 (*ibid* p140). All this points to disruption in the area in the late fourth century.

South West Britain in the Fifth Century

The fifth century in Britain is one of huge change. At the start the Romans are still, just about, in charge, though they were soon to leave. By the end of the century an Anglo-Saxon presence was well established, following a rebellion generally dated to the middle of the century. The effect of this on South West Britain was very different in its different parts. By 500AD we can identify a Saxon presence well into Wiltshire, whereas this had not spread to the rest of the region by then. As Eagles says 'in comparison with the *civitates* of the Atrebates and the Belgae, the material culture and archaeology of the Durotriges could not look more different in the fifth century' (Eagles 2018 p 43).

The main historical source for the fifth century is *De Excidio Britanniae (On The Fall of Britain)* by the Cleric, Gildas. This was written in Latin in the middle of the sixth century, when the events it describes were still sufficiently recent to give the account some credibility. It is important because it is the only surviving historical narrative written by a Briton reasonably close to the events that it describes. Indeed, in the early eighth Century Bede drew heavily upon it for his account of the events of the fifth century in his *Historia Ecclesiastica*. Other historical accounts of the period have been written, but invariably these were composed much later, and are therefore much further from the events they describe. Having said that, Gildas's work reads more like a sermon than an historical treatise, criticising contemporary kings and church people of Britain for their lack of Christian zeal and portraying the coming of the Saxon invaders as God's retribution for their deficiencies. It is thus not a wholly objective account of events, and also suffers from the fact that it gives hardly any dates for the events it recounts, but it nonetheless gives us a picture of the fifth and early sixth centuries that is better than anything else we have. Gildas is thought to have written *De Excidio* around 540 in what is now southern England or at least to have a better knowledge of southern England (Dark 1994 pp 258-266, Eagles 2018 p13, Malim 2020 p 31) although ancient biographies place his birth in Scotland near the Clyde.

Gildas vividly describes the period immediately after the departure of the Romans as one of chaos, with famine and plague prevalent. He pictures a people unable to deal with external threats from the Picts and the Scots, who had to turn to Rome to sort it out. The Emperor sent a legion once, which defeated the invaders. He told the British to build a wall linking the two seas to keep the invaders out, but 'it was ... made of turf not stone so it did no good' (Gildas 15). This reference has puzzled scholars. It appears to have got the timing wrong to be Hadrian's Wall or the Antonine Wall and it was built of turf. But it does acknowledge extensive walls or banks as a recognised military solution to the problems of the day. A second wall, seemingly built 'properly' and running from 'sea to sea' is then referred to, but the invaders returned. Gildas sums up the plight of the British people in the following terms: 'It was weak in beating off the weapons of the enemy but strong in putting up with civil war' (Gildas 22).

Gildas and Bede describe the arrival in Britain of a Germanic people from outside the empire, whom Bede describes as 'Angles, Saxons and Jutes'. Initially they came at the invitation of the British King, Vortigern, as mercenaries, known as *foederati,* to defend Britain from raiders who would have included some of their compatriots. They then rebelled, leading to large parts of Eastern England coming under Saxon control. This all happened, according to Gildas, after the British had appealed to the Roman official, Aëtius, whom Gildas terms 'thrice consul', thus dating the appeal to between 446 and 454. Bede dates it to shortly after Marcian became emperor in 449. Thus, the rebellion must have taken place around 450.

The Britons fought back and secured victories, including most notably at Mount Badon, or *Mons Badonicus,* in which Ambrosius Aurelianus inflicted great slaughter upon the Anglo-Saxons. Ambrosius is mentioned by Gildas in glowing terms, which is unusual for him. He says:

> So that they (The British) should not be entirely destroyed, they take up arms under the command of Ambrosius Aurelianus, a modest man, who perhaps alone of the Roman people had survived such a storm, even though his parents, of course robed in purple, had been killed in the same catastrophe. His descendants, in our time, have failed to live up to their ancestor's greatness but, under Ambrosius, the Britons challenged their previously victorious enemy and, with the Lord's assent, won (Gildas *De Excidio* 25 from Laycock 2009 p89).

This tells us that Ambrosius was the son of parents who held high office but had been killed presumably by the Anglo-Saxon invaders. He is described as being of 'the Roman people', implying that Roman ways were still being followed in his time. Gildas does give a date for this event, but even here he gives it in such an obscure way that it has perplexed scholars ever since. He says of the date: 'that was the year of my birth, as I know, one month of the forty-fourth year since then has already passed'. Scholars agree that this would date the battle to around 500. The Venerable Bede also refers to the battle, implying that it took place 44 years after the arrival of the Saxons (Bede I.16), which would still date it to about 500. After this was a generation of peace with the country divided by an agreed frontier. However, civil war among the Britons continued. (Gildas 26, Eagles 2018 15).

There has been much debate about the location of Mount Badon. This is summed up in a report of Excavations at Liddington Castle near Swindon, believed to be one of the candidates due to the proximity of the village of Badbury and, a little further away, the village of Baydon. The excavation was led by Susan Hirst and Philip Rahtz in 1976 but was not published until 1993. They concluded that Liddington Castle was not the site of Mount Badon, but that the site was likely to be in the South West, with Bath and Badbury Rings, near Wimborne in Dorset, being the leading contenders. Thus, it could be of relevance to Wansdyke (Hirst et al 1993).

This provides an overview of the fifth century from one of the few surviving written sources. I will now look at what archaeology from the wider area can tell us.

Somerset in the Fifth Century

Somerset began the fifth century divided between the *civitates* of the Durotriges in the centre, probably the Belgae in the north and the Dumnonii in the west. We can assume that it carried on that way for a time. There is evidence for activity continuing into the early years of the fifth century in towns such as *Lindinis* (Ilchester), the chief town of the northern Durotriges, Camerton, Charlton, near Shepton Mallet, Gatcombe and the Somerset Levels (Costen 2011 pp8-9).

However, significant changes were on the way, which manifest themselves in the archaeological record in the second half of the fifth century. In that period we start to see the reoccupation of Iron Age hillforts in Somerset and Dorset. Chief among these were Cadbury Castle at South Cadbury, Cadbury Congresbury, near Weston super Mare and Ham Hill, Stoke sub Hamdon. Cadbury Castle and Cadbury Congresbury have both been the subject of classic excavations.

South Cadbury was excavated in the 1960s and 1970s by Leslie Alcock, capturing the public's imagination at the time by suggestions that it might have been the site of King Arthur's Camelot. This showed that the site had been reoccupied in the late fifth and sixth centuries and had been significantly refurbished during that time. A rampart, estimated to have required an astonishing 20km of timber, had been constructed over the earth banks. Inside, the most notable building was a large, rectangular hall built of timber. Imported Mediterranean and Frankish pottery and Germanic glass were found, particularly associated with the hall. This is seen as evidence that this was a high status building of political and/or military importance, used by the elite of the period. The construction of the ramparts was a major undertaking, which seems likely to have been well beyond the resources of the local inhabitants and to have required a considerable amount of organisation (Higham 1992 p93, Dark 2000 pp145-147, Eagles 2018 p36).

Cadbury-Congresbury was investigated by Philip Rahtz and Ian Burrow between 1968 and 1973. Again, the evidence is that the site was in use during the fifth and sixth centuries, maybe as late as

650. Rectangular timber structures were dated to the late fifth century before the arrival of imported pottery and glass, when Roman artefacts and building materials may still have been in use. Significant finds of Mediterranean imported pottery and glass were found. Finds of crucibles and hearths were evidence of the work of jewellers on the site. Like South Cadbury, this is also evidence of an elite settlement. (Dark 2000 pp 132-140, Eagles 2018 p37).

As we have seen in Chapter 2, a number of other Iron Age hillforts in Somerset and Dorset may have been reoccupied at this time.

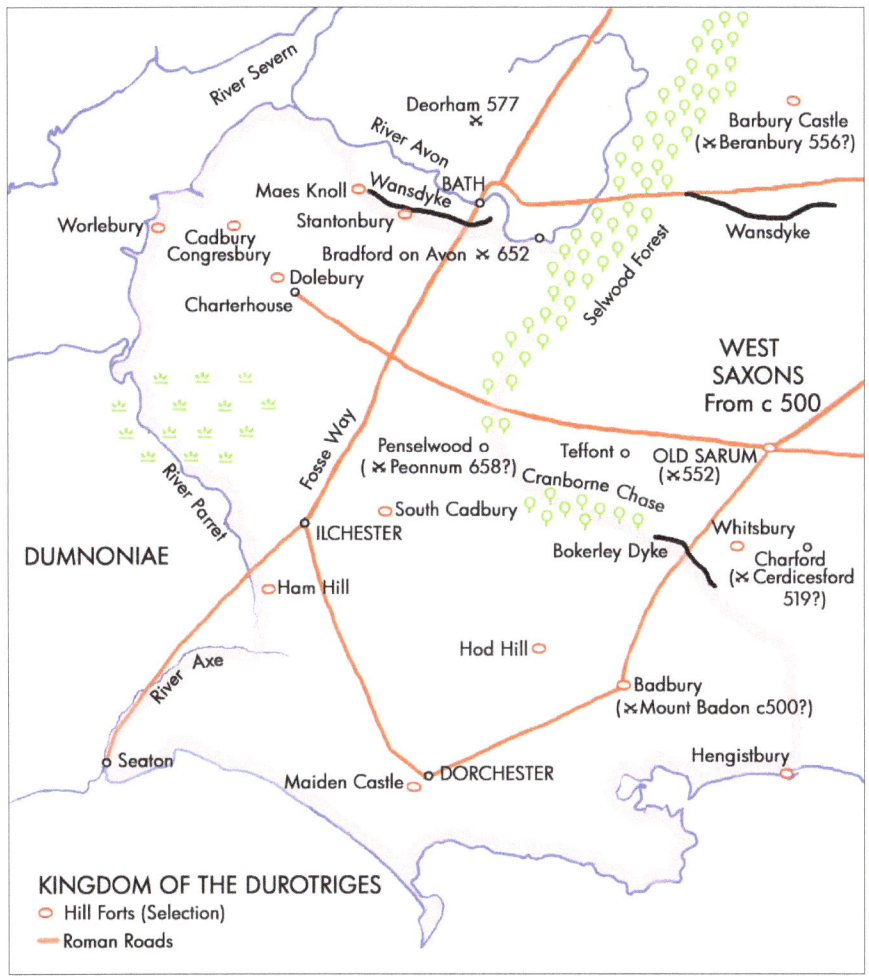

Suggested extent of the Kingdom of the Durotriges, c. 450 to 650. Contains OS data © Crown copyright Open Data 2005.

The key factor is not the reoccupation of the hillforts alone, but the evidence alongside this of high status pottery and glass imported from the Mediterranean and elsewhere. This has also been found at Ham Hill and Glastonbury (Costen 2011 p 17, Eagles 2018 p 35). It does not occur in what is now Dorset, but only further south west in what are now Devon and Cornwall, most noticeably at Tintagel, which seems to have been the main port of entry for these imported goods.

Cadbury Congresbury was very much part of this trading zone, indeed Costen sees it as the pre-eminent settlement in the area by the end of the fifth century and into the sixth (Costen 2011 p 20). This lies in what would previously been the territory of the Belgae. Eagles cites this as evidence that this area was now linked into a trade network which included Devon and Cornwall and no longer belonged to the Belgae. Most likely it had become part of the territory of the Durotriges in the mid 5th Century (Eagles 2018 p36).

Eagles suggests that the Forest of Selwood would have formed the eastern boundary of this territory as part of the settlement following the Battle of Mount Badon. He notes that the Roman Road from the Mendips to Old Sarum was one of those that fell into disuse, and this would have passed through Selwood. The line of West Wansdyke would have been the northern extent this new or expanded territory. However, Bath appears to have become detached from this territory, being on the north side of Wansdyke (Eagles 2018 pp 36-7 and 43-4).

It has been suggested that the Kingdom of Dumnonia, based on Cornwall and Devon, extended into Somerset and Dorset, but Dark dismisses this suggestion. The embanked hut group known as the 'round', the distinctive settlement type of Dumnonia at this time, does not extend west of the Rivers Dart and Parret (Dark 2000 p151). Burial customs of the period also show a distinct difference east and west of the Parret. East of the Parret cemeteries were characterised by east-west extended inhumation burials laid approximately in rows whereas west of the Parret cemeteries tended to have internal foci and features such as burial surrounds (Dark 2000 p117).

Ken Dark has also demonstrated that clear cultural differences between the areas north and south of West Wansdyke began to emerge during the late fifth century. The importation of Mediterranean pottery ceases north of the River Avon. By contrast, grass tempered pottery, which is considered to be distinctively British, is rare in Somerset and Dorset and does not occur north of Gloucestershire, but is common in that county. In other words it is essentially confined to what in Roman times would have been the *civitas* of the Dobunni (Dark 2000 p 134). Also, there is only one significant reoccupied hillfort north of Wansdyke, Crickley Hill near Cheltenham. This seems different in character to the Somerset hillforts, being a palisaded enclosure rather than a structure based on earthen banks. It does not contain imported pottery or glass, or the evidence of jewellery-making evident in the reoccupied hillforts to the south (*ibid* p 146).

Wiltshire in the Fifth Century
A Saxon presence begins to be seen in Wiltshire in the late fifth century, but may not indicate Saxon control. Saxon cemeteries of the fifth century have been identified on the eastern edges of the county. A group of Anglo-Saxon cemeteries from the late fifth century occurs in south east Wiltshire, at Petersfinger, Harnham and Winterbourne Gunner, continuing into the sixth century. A cemetery of similar date has been found at Blacknall Field, Pewsey, which has been argued to be in a frontier area with the Britons (Eagles 2018 p103-4).

Less easy to explain is the early Saxon settlement and adjoining cemetery at Market Lavington, which is dated to the late fifth century. This is right in the centre of the county and well to the west of any other Anglo-Saxon sites of the time. It is thought to be an 'immigrant' community set up in what was essentially still an area controlled by the British. There are parallels for this elsewhere in Somerset, Dorset and the Midlands. The cemetery did not appear to have a strongly military character, suggesting that this was not an invading war band, and burials included men, women and children. The initial date of the Market Lavington burials coincides with the establishment of other Saxon sites mainly on the eastern fringes of the county (Eagles 2001 pp 210 & 217). Draper considers that the analysis of grave goods in these early Saxon burials makes most sense when seen in terms of an emergent, largely native post-Roman society, forging a new distinct cultural identity, albeit under Saxon influence, rather than simply Germanic migrants settling in the region (Draper 2006 p 41).

It must be assumed that, prior to that, political units based on the former Roman *civitates* continued in being. This would indicate the

Dobunni in the north, the Belgae in the centre and south, the Atrebates on the eastern fringes and the Durotriges in the south west corner (Eagles 2018 Paper 1).

The Battle of Guoloph

Now we will turn to an episode which will add a little colour and hopefully some light to this account. It concerns the battle of Guoloph, a brief reference to which occurs in the *Historia Brittonum* of Nennius. It allows us to introduce two of the characters from Gildas's *De Excidio,* and, if true, demonstrates that tribal conflict was alive and well well into the fifth century. The *Historia Brittonum* was written probably in North Wales in the ninth century. Unfortunately, it is not the most reliable of sources. Some of it can only be described as mythology, but the references to the Battle of Guoloph, and its two main protagonists, Ambrosius and Vitalinus, are brief and sober, and not obviously embroidered, so may be given some credence (Laycock 2009 pp46-7).

We start with Vortigern, the *superbus tyrannus* of Gildas, and also the 'luckless king' who first invited the Anglo-Saxons into Britain. Laycock argues that he was the leader of a confederation of the Dobunni and the Cornovi, the Roman *civitas* covering the north west Midlands and north east Wales, which was later rebranded as Powys. Vortigern clearly had Welsh origins but also had among his antecedents one Gloui, who may link him to Gloucester in Dobunnic territory. He also had among his antecedents Guital and Guitolin (in Latin *Vitalis* and *Vitalianus*), who may link him to Vitalinus of the Battle of Guoloph, who we otherwise know nothing about. Another reference in the *Historia Brittonum* tells us that Vortigern was in fear of Ambrosius (Laycock 2009 pp 47-49).

Which brings us to the battle. The name Guoloph is generally held to refer to the Hampshire villages of Over, Middle and Nether Wallop between Andover and Salisbury, and close to the major hillfort of Danebury. As such, it would have been in Atrebatic or Belgic territory. The *Historia* also dates the battle, although somewhat ambiguously, 'From the . . . reign of Vortigern to the quarrel between Vitalinus and Ambrosius are twelve years, that is Wallop, the battle of Wallop' (Nennius p39).

From this reference, the battle has variously been dated to 437 and 458 (Vermaat 1999b). For our purposes, the precise date does not matter. The account is one of a conflict which may very well be between the Dobunni and the Atrebates and/or the Belgae in the middle of the fifth century. Laycock suggests that Ambrosius may have been the leader of the 'Atrebatic' part of the *civitas* of the Belgae (Laycock 2009 pp95-6). This is very much relevant to Wansdyke, in fact the route from the Dobunnic capital of Cirencester to Wallop would pass right through Wansdyke. This is consistent with the model of inter-tribal conflict for the construction of Wansdyke, albeit at a slightly later date than we have considered previously.

Anglo-Saxons in the Upper Thames Valley
Finally, in our review of the fifth century, we need to consider the suggestion of Fowler and others that Wansdyke was constructed as a defence against the Anglo-Saxons who had established themselves early in the fifth century in the Upper Thames Valley around the Oxfordshire village of Dorchester-on-Thames.

It is well attested that there was a significant Anglo-Saxon presence in the area around Dorchester-on-Thames in the early fifth century, known as the *Gewissae* – The 'Reliable Ones'. Finds of early fifth century metalwork and the location of Anglo-Saxon cemeteries from this period are generally located in an area bounded by a line from the Wash to the upper Thames and then along the Thames enclosing what we would now call East Anglia, the South East Midlands and the northern Home Counties. There is a notable cluster around the Upper Thames Valley (Dark 2000 pp 11 and 49).

It has always been something of a puzzle as to what these people were doing there in a relatively isolated group so far from the sea. Laycock proposes that these were *foederati*, mercenaries in the pay of the Catuvellauni, and that they were located here partly because it was a strategic location where the Icknield Way crossed the Thames but also because this was disputed territory between the Catuvellauni and the Dobunni, which had a long history going way back into the days of the Roman Empire. Both were powerful British 'kingdoms' and friction between them was inevitable. The Germanic people were the 'go-to-guys' when you wanted extra resources to defend yourself, as the Romans had done before them and Vortigern was to do at about this time with Hengest and Horsa (Laycock 2009 pp 174 et seq.).

Unlike Vortigern's experience, there is no evidence that these Saxons rebelled. It seems that the Catuvellaunian Kingdom lasted well into the sixth century. Dark shows, on the basis of 'holes' in the distribution of Anglo-Saxon cemeteries in the fifth and sixth centuries, that there could well have been a continuing Romano-British enclave well into this period, a theory first proposed by Sir Mortimer Wheeler in the 1930s. The area includes modern day Oxfordshire stretching east across to the coast in Suffolk and Essex, as well as north Hampshire. The area is ringed with areas where Anglo-Saxon burials have been found, suggesting that these were indicative of communities there to defend the area they surrounded (Dark 2000 pp 97-100). This is consistent with the evidence from the Anglo-Saxon Chronicle that indicates a British presence in this area until 571 when the British were defeated at *Bedcanford,* usually regarded as Bedford, and lost the towns of Limbury, Aylesbury, Benson and Eynsham, all of which would have been in Catuvellaunian territory *(ASC pp 18-19).* If the *foederati* had rebelled the kingdom would not have survived in British hands. So we must conclude that these were not Anglo-Saxons with hostile intent unless it was at the behest of their Catuvellaunian employers. Moreover, the Dobunni were probably the main preoccupation of the Catuvellauni in this area.

The map below illustrates a number of issues that make the suggestion that Wansdyke was built to defend against these Anglo-Saxons unsatisfactory. First, the Upper Thames Valley is some distance

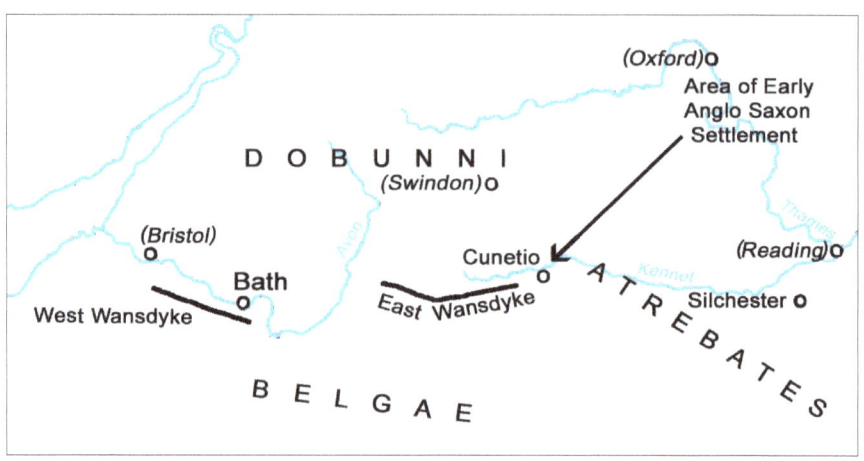

Line of attack from Thames Valley. Contains OS data © Crown copyright Open Data 2005.

from Wansdyke, and the advancing forces would have to pass through Dobunnic or Atrebatic territory on the way. Either of these groups were potentially hostile to the Catuvellauni. Second, Wansdyke faces in the wrong direction. The direction of attack would be from the north east. It is possible that attackers would use the Ridgeway, but it is equally possible to outflank the earthwork completely by coming round its eastern end. Thirdly, this scenario offers no model for the construction of West Wansdyke which is nowhere near the point of attack envisaged. In my view we need to look elsewhere for the explanation.

Fifth Century - Conclusion
We need to consider the fifth century in two parts. The first half of the century shows characteristics of a 'post-Roman' period, where the polities and many of the issues had not changed since Roman times. Gildas makes a number of references to ongoing conflicts, and the period seems to have been quite unstable. This instability could well have had its seeds in the last years of the Roman occupation. This allows us to define a period from about 370 to 450 when there was conflict and Wansdyke would have been on the border between the Dobunni and the Belgae.

After about 450 we start to see what are now Somerset and Wiltshire developing in very different ways. In Somerset we see reoccupation of hillforts and the importation of Mediterranean pottery, which is not seen in Dorset or Wiltshire, but shows links to Devon and Cornwall. The Belgae seem to have been ousted from north Somerset by this time. Eagles argues that Selwood Forest would have marked the eastern extent of this area, possibly as the line of partition agreed following the Battle of Mount Badon. Meanwhile, Wiltshire is starting to come under the influence of the Anglo-Saxons, late in the century, and seemingly coming from the east, which does not seem to fit with a north facing frontier.

The period from 450 onwards does not seem a very promising period for advancing the case for a north facing frontier.

The Sixth and Seventh Centuries - The Coming of The Saxons
By the end of the fifth Century both Somerset and much of Wiltshire remained under British control, with such Anglo-Saxon presence as

there was mainly in Wiltshire and not at this stage in control of territory. They may have been *foederati* with their families or immigrant settlers or, indeed, possibly British people who had adopted Germanic customs. This was soon to change.

The Anglo-Saxon Chronicle – An 'Origin Myth for Wessex'?
The Anglo-Saxon Chronicle gives an account of the coming of the West Saxons in the early sixth century, which provides a starting point, though a controversial one. The Chronicle was first compiled in the late 9th Century at the Court of King Alfred. This is 350 to 400 years after the event for the late 5th and early 6th centuries, and it is seriously questioned how accurate it could be for this period at a time when written records may have been few and far between and it has been suggested that aural records would be unreliable beyond 200 years into the past. Furthermore, it was not an attempt to record history objectively but a propaganda exercise for the kings of Wessex, with the result that its compilers could be selective in what they recorded and would embellish the facts when it suited them. Accordingly Dark rejects it as a source of evidence, Eagles refers to it as an 'origin myth' while Laycock sees no reason to reject it out of hand provided it is used with caution (Dark 2000 p43, Eagles 2001 p 204, Laycock 2009 pp 183-5).

The Chronicle shows its most perverse side in describing exactly the events we are interested in: the coming of Cerdic, described as the founder of the kingdom of Wessex. This event seems to be recorded twice, once in 495, where Cerdic and his son Cynric are explicitly named and once in 514 where there is a general reference to the arrival of the Saxons and to two other characters, Stuff and Whitgar. On both occasions they landed at a place called *Cerdicesora*, thought to be somewhere near Southampton. In between, in 508, Cerdic and Cynric had killed a British king and his army. Then in 519, we are told that Cerdic and Cynric undertook the government of the West Saxons and in the same year they fought the British at *Cerdicesford,* thought to be Charford, on the present-day boundary of Wiltshire and Hampshire. It says 'And the Royal Family of the West Saxons ruled from that day on' (*ASC* pp 16-17). For our purposes, there is no reason to become embroiled in the discrepancies over the earlier dates. The events of 519 seem to be the ones that matter. They represent the beginnings of the

West Saxon kingdom and the entry of Cerdic and Cynric into what is today Wiltshire.

We can also take from this that the West Saxons came from the south and gradually advanced north over a period of years. Battles with the British are recorded at the unidentified *Cerdicesley* in 527, Old Sarum in 552 and *Beranbyrg,* thought to be Barbury Castle near Swindon, in 556 (*ASC* pp 16-17).

This brings us to Ceawlin, the one West Saxon king to be described by Bede as a *bretwalda,* which indicates a kind of 'super-king' who had power beyond his home territory. He was said by the *Chronicle* to be Cynric's son but may actually have been his grandson (*ASC 685,* Matthews p139), and he is first mentioned in the Anglo-Saxon Chronicle entry for 556, where he fought alongside Cynric against the Britons at *Beranbyrg.* Given its location the opponents were probably the Dobunni. We are told that he became the leader of the West Saxons in 560, and that he fought a number of battles over a wide area during his thirty year reign. The locations of these battles are *Wibbandun* (location unknown, possibly Wimbledon, 568), where he pursued Ethelbert into Kent, *Deorham,* thought to be Dyrham, north of Bath (577), where Ceawlin and Cuthwin defeated three kings and took from them the cities of Gloucester, Cirencester and Bath, *Fethanleag,* thought to be Stoke Lyne in Oxfordshire (584) and *Wodnesbeorg* (592). All of these seem to be north of Wansdyke except *Wodnesbeorg,* which is, as we know, almost on Wansdyke (Laycock 2008 p216, Eagles 2001 p205).

The description of the battle of *Wodnesbeorg* in the Chronicle is confusing. We are told that there was a great slaughter of Britons, but that Ceawlin was driven from his kingdom. This has led to speculation that there were two West Saxon kingdoms in competition with each other, whose boundary lay along Wansdyke (Eagles 2001 p 205). These would comprise the Cerdicings who had moved up from the south and the Gewissae of the Upper Thames Valley who had been victorious at *Bedcanford.* This, in turn, led the Foxes to suggest that Ceawlin was the builder of East Wansdyke. However, the Chronicle tells us that Ceawlin died the year after the battle, so he would have had little time to build it.

Another theory is that Ceawlin was not an Anglo-Saxon at all, but a Briton. All the early kings of the founding dynasty, the descendants of Cerdic, have British names, all beginning with 'c'. Rupert Matthews argues that Ceawlin was trying to establish himself as a latter-day *tyrannus superbus,* a successor to Vortigern and Ambrosius, and this was the context for the large number of battles fought by him, and his uncle Cuthwulf at *Bedcanford* (Bedford). This would also explain how south Gloucestershire remained in British hands after the defeat of the three kings at *Deorham* as the archaeology appears to show (see below). Matthews also argues that the battle of *Wodnesbeorg* was fought in 592 between Ceawlin and his nephew Coel, who we learn ruled for five years from 591. This would explain how Ceawlin was driven out, after apparently winning the battle – he may have lost it! Matthews then argues that Coel had formed an alliance with the Gewissae to achieve the victory, and that he now made this alliance permanent as the beginnings of Wessex (Matthews 2012). Whether this explains why kings of Wessex continued to have British names after this time and whether the Anglo-Saxon Chronicle would have given such prominence to a British dynasty is less certain.

This all seems a little confusing, and I have barely mentioned King Arthur, who would have been active around 500 and is traditionally associated with the Battle of Mount Badon! I make no apologies for dealing with it at some length as it introduces us to some of the characters and is very much part of the backstory. Eagles' suggestion that we treat it as an 'origin myth' for Wessex seems a sound suggestion.

As we go into the seventh century, the Chronicle seems to become more coherent, and there are events it records for this century that are important to the narrative. The first of these occurred in 628 when Cynegils and Cwichelm of the West Saxons fought against Penda of Mercia at Cirencester, and were defeated. They settled on Penda's terms. Mercia was now the dominant power (Eagles 2018 p 102). The Foxes thought that this settlement could have been the trigger for the construction of West Wansdyke, citing a Saxon burial at Camerton as evidence of a Saxon presence to the south by then. There would then have been seven years of paganism, within which Wansdyke could have been built according to the Foxes (Fox and Fox 1960 p 43).

This reference to 'seven years of paganism' brings us to an event that has been central to the discussion about Wansdyke, the baptism of Cynegils, King of Wessex, said by the Anglo-Saxon Chronicle to have taken place at Dorchester-on-Thames in 635 (*ASC* pp 26-27). This was

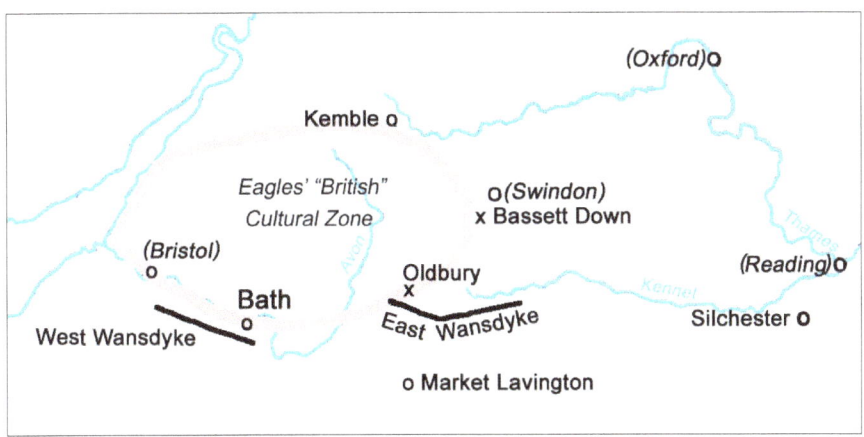

Eagles' suggested British cultural zone extending into 7th century. Contains OS data © Crown copyright Open Data 2005.

the start of the conversion of Wessex to Christianity. As we have seen in the previous chapter, many archaeologists and historians traditionally argued that Wansdyke could not have been built after this date because of its pagan name, but this position has now been refuted.

The final 'marker' from the *Chronicle* that we will examine from the seventh century is the Battle of *Peonnum* of 658. Here Cenwahl drove the Welsh (ie The British) 'in flight as far as the Parret'. This describes the conquest of Somerset by the Kingdom of Wessex. *Peonnum* is usually taken to be Penselwood (the head of Selwood) near where the present day counties of Wiltshire, Somerset and Dorset meet. It was the beginning of the end of the Durotriges, or their successors, as a British kingdom, and gives rise to a different set of scenarios for Wansdyke (*ASC* p 32).

It can be seen that the *Chronicle* has given us a framework for the sixth and seventh centuries, better for the seventh than the sixth. We now need to see how this compares with the archaeological record.

Archaeology
The archaeological evidence shows that by the end of the sixth century the Saxons occupied the east and centre of Wiltshire. Up to that point Saxon burials occur as far west as Teffont and Warminster. They are absent from the far south west of the county, ie the Cranborne Chase area, at this time, indicating that this was still part of a British kingdom, which we have seen above is likely to be that of the Durotriges. In the

north west, Saxon finds are sparse though finds are found as far west as Kemble, on the Gloucestershire border, Charlton, near Malmesbury and West Ashton, near Trowbridge. There is evidence of a British presence continuing in the north west of the county and what is now south Gloucestershire in an area bounded by Kemble, West Ashton, Bath and the River Severn until some time in the seventh century. A particularly significant find was a Celtic hanging-bowl from Seagry, while there is a noticeable lack of early Anglo-Saxon burials and artefacts of the late sixth or early seventh century in north west Wiltshire and South Gloucestershire. Additional support is found in the exceptional number of Brittonic place names in north west Wiltshire, with the suggestion that Kemble was on an internal division of the Dobunni. This situation appears to have changed little by the late seventh century. (Eagles 2018 p143 *et seq* and Figs 10 & 11).

In medieval times West Ashton was within the bounds of the Forest of Selwood. A line from Kemble to West Ashton if continued south would run right down the middle of the Forest, already argued to be the eastern limit of the Durotriges in north Somerset. Indeed, it seems likely that the whole of this line would have been part of the great forest, certainly known to the Saxons in the 9th century, that extended from the Thames Valley to Blackmore Vale in Dorset. This comprised what would later become the Forests of Braydon, Chippenham, Melksham and Selwood in Medieval times, and would have formed a significant natural boundary (VCH p391 *et seq*, Eagles 2018 p145).

To the immediate east of this boundary is the 'small shire' of the *Canningas*. Small shires are a feature of the early development of Wessex, being areas smaller than a county, which predated the formation of the counties in the ninth or tenth centuries, and possibly emerged from the Roman *pagi*. Most of those that have been identified are in the east of Wessex – Hampshire, Surrey and Berkshire. The *Canningas*, derived from Old English, the people of Canna, give the parishes of Bishops Cannings and All Cannings their names. The area is thought to extend to both sides of Wansdyke (Reynolds 2005 p174, Eagles 2018 p116). In this area are a number of high status Anglo-Saxon burials of the late seventh century including what was thought to be a bed-burial of a female at Roundway Down, but these are the most westerly Anglo-Saxon finds from this period (Eagles 2018 p116).

In Somerset, finds of Anglo-Saxon jewellery and other items from the first half of the sixth century have occurred, particularly on the coast. The interpretation is that this is the take up of novel 'Saxon' fashions by Britons in the area (Eagles 2018 p139). It should be remembered that Cadbury Congresbury was still occupied at this time and its occupants had a taste for exotic possessions.

As we have seen, The *Anglo-Saxon Chronicle* tells us that Cenwahl fought at *Peonnum* in 658 and drove the Welsh back to the Parret. A further entry in 682 describes Centwine putting the Britons to flight as far as the sea. This seems to be the end of over 250 years of what is now Somerset as a post-Roman, British kingdom. Now grants of land by Kings of Wessex and the church in this area start to be recorded. Centwine is said to have granted six hides to Glastonbury Abbey when he appointed a new abbot in 678, and two further charters followed. King Ine of Wessex (688-726) granted further charters to both Glastonbury and Muchelney Abbeys and played a major role in the development of Glastonbury (Costen 2011 pp 188-190, Eagles 2018 p35). In 705, the *Chronicle* tells us that the diocese of Sherborne was founded to serve the land 'west of the wood' (ie Selwood) with Aldhelm as its first bishop *(ASC p40)*. Sherborne had a British predecessor, *Lanprobi,* and Cenwahl was said to have transferred a 100 hide estate from the British monastery to the new diocese in 671 (Eagles 2018 p139). We can conclude from this that Somerset was firmly under the control of Wessex by the late seventh century, and the kings of Wessex were working hard to strengthen their control.

Sixth and Seventh Centuries – Conclusion

For much of this period the north–south divide between what are now Wiltshire and Somerset stayed in place. This followed the line of the Forest of Selwood and may well be along the line agreed following Mount Badon. The West Saxons strengthened their control over most of Wiltshire, while the Durotriges, or their successors, continued as a 'late antique' Romano-British kingdom. Not until the second half of the seventh century did Wessex finally make a move against the Durotriges to bring it under their control.

The significance for Wansdyke is that there are clearly no scenarios that will explain the building of the entire structure during this period.

They would have to be built at separate times to counter separate threats. We have examined a couple of these: the Battle of *Wodnesbeorg* in 592 as the trigger to build East Wansdyke and the defeat of Wessex by Mercia in 628 as the trigger for building West Wansdyke.

It is not clear how threatened the Durotriges felt by their neighbours to the east, but that was where the threat eventually came from, and a north facing bank was of no value in that situation. I tend to the view that it was unlikely that Wansdyke was built during this period.

Wessex and Mercia - 660 to 900

Conflict between the Anglo-Saxon Kingdoms of Wessex and Mercia had been onging since at least 628, when, as we have seen, Penda had defeated Wessex at Cirencester. It would provide the context for this area until the early ninth century. This is a new strand to our story. To examine it we need to place greater reliance on the *Anglo-Saxon Chronicle*. While archaeology has served us well in comparing finds from British and Saxon sources it is much less effective in comparing artefacts from two different Anglo-Saxon kingdoms. Also, we are coming much closer to the *Chronicle's* date of compilation, so its reliability is improving, and there are now other written sources to back it up. One thing that is helpful is the study of surviving charters, usually detailing the transfer of land. These occur in increasing numbers in this period, and we have already looked at the Alton Priors Charter of 825 and the Stanton St Bernard Charter of 903, which give us a possible and a definite end-date for construction of Wansdyke respectively.

Penda, the King of Mercia from around 626 to 655 was a committed pagan at a time when Christianity was rapidly taking hold elsewhere. As king of the central part of the country, he spent much of his time fighting with the kingdoms around him, Northumbria, East Anglia and Wessex, and he was preoccupied with Northumbria and East Anglia during much of his reign.

However, an incident with Cenwahl of Wessex is recorded in 645. Cenwahl had rejected his wife, who was Penda's sister. In revenge, Penda attacked him and forced him into exile in East Anglia for three years (*ASC* pp 26-27 and 32-33). It was after Cenwahl's return that the Battle of *Penselwood* was fought, but nothing more of the ongoing conflict between Wessex and Mercia is recorded until the reign of Wulfhere,

Penda's son, who in 661 fought Cenwahl at the unidentified Pontesbury and pursued him to Ashdown, the chalk downlands of Berkshire and Wiltshire, very much in the vicinity of Wansdyke. Wulfere eventually fought his way to the Isle of Wight. In doing so he may have bypassed the core areas of Wessex - Wiltshire and Hampshire - but took control of Surrey and Sussex en route. By the 670s Wulfhere probably controlled much of the south of England including Wessex, whose kings may well have had the role of sub-kings at that time (Yorke 1995 p 66). Wessex seemed to recover, and by 674 or 675 Escwine, who by the time was king of Wessex, fought against Wulfhere at *Biedanheafde* (*ASC* p 34-35). The conflicts between Wulfhere and Wessex at this time provide a possible scenario for the construction of Wansdyke. However, by the 680s Caedwalla, the King of Wessex, was retaking territory formerly held by Mercia in the Isle of Wight and Surrey (Yorke 1995 p66, Reynolds and Langlands 2006 p36).

Moving on to the eighth century, the period between 710 and around 730, during the reign of King Ine and his successor Aethelheard, saw a series of internal rebellions in Wessex. Possibly taking advantage of this, Ine was attacked by Ceolred of Mercia in 715 at *Wodnesbeorge*. Then in 733, the Mercians struck again, this time at Somerton, deep in Somerset. From then until the battle of *Beorhtford* in 752 Mercia may have ruled Wessex directly. After that Wessex may have got back some independence briefly but probably remained under the control of Mercia until the beginning of the ninth century (Yorke 1995 p 62, Zaluckyj 2001 p135-7). King Cynewulf of Wessex may have gained some territory from Mercia but was defeated by Offa of Mercia at Bensington or Benson in Oxfordshire in 779, after which Offa appears to have taken control of Berkshire. Beortric, the king of Wessex from 786 to 802, seems to have been under the control of Mercia, but on the very day that Egbert succeeded him in 802 the men of Wiltshire won a battle against the Hwicce, a sub-kingdom of Mercia, at Kempsford and this seems to have begun to turn the tide in Wessex's favour. Certainly, north Wiltshire and Somerset seem to have been regained by Wessex on a permanent basis from this date (Yorke 1995 pp 63-64).

The grant of land charters can add some corroboration to these accounts. With Mercia in the ascendency at this time, the key is to look for grants of land in Wessex which required the consent of the Mercian king of the time and those that did not. Grants to the abbeys of Bath and Malmesbury are particularly significant because they both lie very much in territory that was contested by the two kingdoms, who vied for influence with grants of land. The nunnery at Bath was founded by the Hwicce in around 675 (Reynolds and Langlands 2006 p36). King Aethelbald of Mercia's consent was required for a grant of land to Glastonbury Abbey in 744 but not for a grant to Malmesbury Abbey in 745. King Cynewulf of Wessex (757-786) was clearly submissive to Offa of Mercia in a charter early in his reign to St Peter's Minster in Bath (Eagles 2018 p162).

Mercia began a period of decline after the death of Coenwulf in 821 from which it never really recovered, and Wessex began to gain the ascendency. Ecgbert of Wessex won a decisive victory against an attack by Beornwulf of Mercia in 825 at *Ellendun,* identified as Wroughton, south of Swindon. He followed this up by an attack on Mercia in 829 and declared himself king of the Mercians. Mercia regained its independence within the year, though the circumstances are unclear (Zaluckyj 2001 pp 232-238). By this time we have reached our possible end date of the Alton Priors Charter of 825. Wessex was at least of equal standing to Mercia by this time and would probably have no need of building defences against them. This remained the case until the Vikings came onto the scene.

By the middle of the ninth century the Danish invasions had begun, and attacking Wessex would have been the last thing on Mercia's mind, indeed they formed an alliance with Wessex for a time to try to resist the Danes. Alfred ascended to the throne of Wessex in 871. His system of defences was based upon the *burh,* the series of defended towns no more than 20 miles (or a day's march) apart. This was a completely different system of defence to the extended earthwork. Although it may have also incorporated defended bridges, herepaths, causeways and look-out or signalling stations (Haslam 2012 p201) there is no evidence that it included strategic earthworks such as Wansdyke. If Alfred had built Wansdyke, Asser, in his *Life of King Alfred,* would have been sure to have told us. He did after all tell us about Offa's Dyke. We can therefore conclude that, even without the evidence of the Alton Priors Charter, it is unlikely that Wansdyke was built after 825. The victory by Wessex at Kempsford in 802 probably allows us to consider this the end-date for practical purposes as this battle seems to have brought the area in which

East Wansdyke was constructed permanently back under the control of Wessex.

We therefore have a period of about 140 years, between about 660 and just after 800 when the context was right for Wansdyke to have been built. Commentators have generally opted for the end of this period. In 1998, Reynolds proposed that it was the result of a short-lived settlement between the West Saxons and the Mercians in the late eighth or early ninth century, which he termed Wessex's equivalent of Offa's Dyke (Reynolds 1999 p85). Draper proposed a late eighth century construction again as defence against the Mercian threat and possibly a launch pad for attacks against them. He saw the two sections of dyke as the northern boundaries of the Sumersaete and the Wilsaete. He regarded the battle of Kempsford as rendering Wansdyke redundant overnight, thus fulfilling Fowler's criteria for the ditch to be unfinished (Draper 2006 p60). More recently, Reynolds has proposed that the relative independence obtained by Cynewulf between 758 and 779 would provide a likely window within which time Wansdyke was constructed (Reynolds 2020 p 273).

Conclusion

The historical context helps considerably to narrow down the likely timeframe within which Wansdyke was constructed.

One of the contenders is the period from, say, 367, the date of the Barbarian Conspiracy, to around 500, the date at which the Saxons began to take control of Wiltshire but not of Somerset. Within this period many commentators favour the late fifth century, but there is also a strong argument for construction by the Belgae, which would have occurred before about 450 when it is postulated that the Durotriges took control of northern Somerset, starting to reoccupy hillforts and seemingly in a trading alliance with the Dumnonii.

Although a pagan Saxon scenario has been suggested for the construction of Wansdyke, this coincides with a period in the sixth and the first half of the seventh century when Wiltshire was under Saxon control while Somerset was still under British control, rendering the scenario unlikely. Sufficient evidence has been advanced to enable us to discount the conversion of Wessex to Christianity in 635 as an end date for the construction of Wansdyke.

Somerset came under Saxon control in about 660 after the battle of *Peonnum*. From this time onwards another set of scenarios is possible. In this case the context is the ongoing conflict between Wessex and Mercia.

The latest possible end-date is 903, the date in which Wansdyke is first mentioned in a charter. I have discounted the period beyond about 825, partly on the grounds that the Alton Priors charter of that date names a dyke, although it could be a forgery, and partly because this more or less coincides with the beginning of the period when Wessex began to gain ascendency over Mercia and therefore would have no need of building the dyke. We can probably also discount the period from 802, when the battle of Kempsford is thought to have permanently re-established control of northern Wiltshire by Wessex.

We can therefore identify two periods when the construction of Wansdyke is most likely to have occurred - first between about 370 and 450 and, second, between about 660 and 800. In the next chapter I will discuss two possible scenarios for the construction of Wansdyke, one from the first period and one from the second, which seek to explain why and when Wansdyke was constructed.

6

Towards a Hypothesis

Out on a windswept hillside a long, long time ago, a snake of people could be seen with their picks and shovels piling up earth from a ditch they were digging to form a long, high bank, gleaming white from the newly exposed chalk, spreading along the hillside as far as the eye could see. What had compelled them to take on this monumental task? Were they in fear of their lives – it didn't look like it - or trying to protect their land from being taken from them? Were they Romans, Welsh or Britons, or the people of Wessex?

We have looked at a period of just over half a millennium, when huge changes were taking place in what we now call England, although it wasn't called that then. We began with the Romans, who despite creating a level of sophistication in society that was arguably not equalled again for a millennium or more, ultimately couldn't hold on to their colony. Not long after this people from northern Europe, who had never been under the Roman yoke, began to take control, introducing very different ways of doing things. In the south west of England they created the Kingdom of Wessex, though it took them over 200 years to extend their kingdom to the 'Severn Sea'. By then they were coming under attack from their northern neighbours from Mercia, an ongoing problem for a century and a half. Then the Mercians, in particular, had to turn their attention to more attacks from northern Europe in the shape of the Vikings.

We have a constantly changing picture, with warfare commonplace, which could have led to many situations where the need for a great boundary was felt. We have narrowed down some of the options, but, in the absence of any good dating evidence, we are still left with a number of scenarios which could explain this enigmatic earthwork. So you will have to settle for a story with multiple endings, from which you can choose the one that works best for you. These scenarios pit Briton against Briton, Briton against Anglo-Saxon and Anglo-Saxon against

Anglo-Saxon. In years to come one, or indeed none, of these options may be proved correct but that is no use to us here and now, as we attempt to reach some sort of closure.

Scenario 1: A Briton versus Briton Conflict at the Collapse of the Roman Empire

In the absence of Rome, Gildas describes a nation that was 'weak in beating off the weapons of the enemy but strong in putting up with civil war and the burden of sin'. 'Kings were anointed not in God's name, but as being crueller than the rest' (Gildas 21). More pragmatically there was a situation where the Romans could no longer guarantee the security of the state or the legal, civil and administrative frameworks that went with it. Ruling elites, whose positions were underpinned by these structures, were vulnerable. The end of the state monopoly on force would have seen the rise of competing 'warlords' (Esmonde Cleary 2011 pp20-1). This breakdown may have occurred before the nominal end of the Roman occupation in 410. This is the basis of the scenario for the construction of Wansdyke as a defensive line and a boundary between two of these warring 'tribes'.

As we have seen, there is certainly evidence for upheaval as early as the final decades of Roman rule. The so-called Barbarian Conspiracy took place in 367 and Cunetio and Gatcombe were refortified at about this time, possibly as a direct response to it. Certainly, works of this magnitude would not have been carried out unless a real need for them was recognised. The series of villa fires we have noted also took place in the late fourth century. We can certainly identify 367 as lying within a period of instability within which Wansdyke could have been built.

The builders of Wansdyke would have been from the Roman *civitas* of the Belgae, or their successors after the Romans left, but who still considered themselves to be Romans. The aggressors from the north would have been the Dobunni or their successors, to whom the same applies. There is a suggestion from Iron Age coin distributions that the Dobunni were the occupiers of north Somerset before the arrival of the Romans, and this would be more than sufficient incentive to launch an attack on the 'interlopers from the south' who had stolen part of their tribal lands. This could have been the motive, while the power vacuum left by the departing Romans would have provided the opportunity.

The Mendip mines had been a valuable resource for the Romans, but now their importance may have significantly diminished. Once the Romans departed, no new coinage was being minted, and buildings had stopped being built with stone with metal accessories. The distance from the *civitas* capital in Winchester may have been becoming more of a problem.

Oldbury Castle from Wansdyke

So we can envisage a situation where the Dobunni had moved against Bath and taken it. This sent shock waves through the Belgae. Quickly, they blocked the Fosse Way, the most likely route an invading force would take to make further incursions into their territory. They were unable to connect to the River Avon, their original frontier, so they built a bank where they could a few miles back. In Wiltshire, Oldbury Castle was a Dobunnic stronghold, gazing, like the eye of Sauron from Mordor, across at the Belgae as they built their bank. But build it they did, and perhaps the Dobunni were less motivated here as the part of Wiltshire south of the dyke may not have been part of their hereditary lands. Once again, the Belgae sought to close the main north-south route along the Ridgeway. Building the bank stopped when they reached Savernake Forest, which belonged to the Atrebates, who, although probably historically allies, could deal with their own problems. They had the fortified town of Cunetio on their boundary with the Dobunni.

Gaps were left, very likely where woodland occurred, which would at least slow down an invader, and could be filled in later. In particular, the Roman Road from Bath to Morgan's Hill was left as it was. Maybe its 'agger' delineated the boundary between the two factions sufficiently clearly. This area was heavily wooded, part of the Great Forest running from Selwood to the Thames. Maybe the River Avon was considered to suffice as a boundary to the west of the wood.

The Romans had the know-how and organisation to build a structure like this. They had built Hadrian's Wall originally as an earth bank, and the Antonine Wall, which still was. They regularly built marching camps while on the move. While there was a new order in Britain, as much of the occupying army had left either with Constantine III or had been recalled to defend Rome, there were still people around who knew how to manage these projects. It needed somebody who could mark out the line, reusing existing banks where they could, and then organise the builders into gangs to build it across varying geology and different land ownerships.

Once the bank was raised it was intended to build gates at strategic crossing points to control traffic, as had been done in a much grander scale on Hadrian's Wall, but it seems the bank was never finished.

If the Belgae had assumed that the threat to their territory came from the north, they were wrong. About 450 the Durotriges emerged out of the Somerset Levels and attacked over the Mendips. They caught the Belgae unawares and soon established themselves in North Somerset. They quickly occupied Cadbury-Congresbury and this became one of their main centres, from which they imported the luxury goods from the Mediterranean and elsewhere which were now becoming available through a trading alliance with the Dumnonii from Cornwall and Devon, who imported them through Tintagel. Links to the south also included South Cadbury and Ham Hill, which were also part of this network.

This changed the political geography. Now, there were two different 'tribes' south of the two stretches of Wansdyke. There is no reason to think that, having just had north Somerset taken off them by the Durotriges, the Belgae would have co-operated with them in building a defence against the Dobunni. So the end date for this scenario would be around 450.

In terms of what we learned in the previous chapter, there are two main issues to address with this scenario. First, did the Belgae occupy north Somerset? If not it is difficult to make the scenario work. Second, there is the issue of parish boundaries preceding the building of the earthwork, which we looked at in Chapter 4. There is no doubt that a scenario that relies on a later date for the drawing of parish boundaries is the more robust. But Desmond Bonney, who originally studied this issue in relation to Wansdyke concluded that some boundaries had had continuous existence since Roman or earlier times. Whether a Roman Road was used as a boundary depended on the extent of Iron-Age occupation, which tended to be denser on the chalk (Bonney 1972 p 183).The apparently ephemeral nature of Wansdyke may also have been a factor in it being ignored by those who defined parish boundaries (Hinton 2017).

West Wansdyke would have been useful to the Durotriges, marking out a northern boundary, and maybe they were content to stay to the south of this line, although Bath would have been tantalisingly close to the north. However, around 500 there was great battle, at a place called Mount Badon. The Britons had got together to fight the incomers from northern Germany and Denmark we now call the Anglo-Saxons. Who formed this alliance? Could it have been the Dobunni getting together with the Durotriges and the Dumnonii, and others from what we now call Wales, to defeat a common enemy? Whoever it was, they were successful, and managed to secure a treaty with the Anglo-Saxons to leave them in peace, a peace which lasted for some time.

We don't know where this battle was fought, but as we have seen, Bath and Badbury Rings in Dorset, are likely candidates. If that was the case, the Saxons were probably stretching themselves a bit. They would not have occupied the area east of Bath by this time, but may have reached Dorset from the south if the Anglo-Saxon Chronicle's account is to be believed.

These kingdoms, for that is most probably what they had now become, based on their hill fort centres, continued to survive and thrive for another 150 years or so, as post-Roman or Romano-British societies. We do not know too much about them. It was an age of saints, and we get a tantalising glimpse into their world when Saint Augustine paid their leaders a visit early in the seventh century, under the oak tree that bore his name, possibly somewhere near Kemble on the Gloucestershire-Wiltshire boundary (Eagles 2018 Chapter 10). His aim was to convert them to his brand of Roman Christianity, and he failed due, it is said by Bede, to his arrogance.

We can picture a remnant of the Dobunni in the area of what is now South Gloucestershire. The northern Durotriges were in north and central Somerset as far south west as the River Parret and Taunton, with the great Forest of Selwood as their eastern boundary. Their southern cousins occupied Dorset, while Cornwall, Devon and West Somerset were occupied by the Dumnonii. And so it stayed until the middle of the seventh century.

We looked at this period in the previous chapter, and concluded that this was a period where scenarios for the building of Wansdyke were difficult, though not impossible, to construct. They would need to postulate the two parts of the earthwork being built at separate times, with the British building West Wansdyke, but, unless it was built before about 500, East Wansdyke being built by the Saxons of Wessex.

So we are going to turn the clock forward to around 660 for the second of our scenarios, the time when Wessex had finally moved against Somerset and annexed it.

Scenario 2: Wessex vs Mercia – c660 to 800
The scenario that has been gaining traction in recent years is that Wansdyke was built by the West Saxons on the boundary with their northern neighbours from Mercia. Warfare between the two was ongoing throughout much of this period from the late seventh century to the beginning of the ninth, as each jockeyed for position, with Mercia generally having the upper hand. This is not a new proposition. We have noted that Leland and Aubrey both proposed that Wansdyke was built to separate Wessex and Mercia. But by the late twentieth century, the favoured view tended to be that it was late-Roman or immediately post-Roman, as outlined above.

We have also noted that there have been several different proposals for when during these 150 years it could have been built. I am going to focus on the most recent proposition, put forward by Andrew Reynolds, that it was built by Cynewulf, King of Wessex, in the period between 757 and 779.

Cynewulf came to power in 757, which is where we take our first date from. The Anglo-Saxon Chronicle tells us that in that year he, together with the *witan*, or council, of the Kingdom 'deprived Sigeberht, his relative, of the kingdom because of his unlawful actions – except for Hampshire' (*ASC* p47). Sigeberht had been king for only a year before being deposed, though retaining Hampshire meant that his downfall was only partial. That downfall was completed soon after, when he murdered his loyal ealdorman, Cumbra, after which Cynewulf drove him away to the Weald, where he was eventually murdered. Cynewulf subsequently reigned for 31 years, and can be counted among the more successful kings of Wessex.

The first thing to note is that Cynewulf did not act alone in this matter, but in consultation with the *witan*. The *witan* clearly had the power to depose a king and were not to be treated lightly. This meant that, at this time, the kingship was effectively an elected position. And what do people newly elected to a position do? They make big promises! Maybe one of those promises was to firm up the frontier of Wessex by delineating it with an earthbank that would also act as a defensive line, and he would call it after one of the founding fathers of his dynasty, Woden (Reynolds 2020 p265).

The second thing to note is that in the same year, Offa became king of Mercia. There is no doubt that Offa was one of the most successful of Mercian kings, indeed probably *the* most successful, and very much of a stature where he was an actor on the European stage, interacting with Charlemagne and the Papacy. He also had a long reign of 39 years. With two powerful men coming to their positions of power at the same time there was bound to be some flexing of muscles to test each other out.

This needs to be seen in the context of events in the recent past. Offa's predecessor, Aethelbald, had invaded deep into Somerset, taking the Royal *vil* of Somerton. He saw fit to dispose of land in the north of Wessex and was a patron of Glastonbury Abbey, which was well within Wessex. At the time of Cynewulf's accession in 757, Wessex was very much on the back foot. One of Cynewulf's first acts as king was to witness a charter of Aethelbald's transferring land in North Wiltshire to Malmesbury Abbey. This was land which would have been considered part of Wessex, as was Malmesbury, and indicated that Cynewulf was told to witness the document, implying that he was subservient to Aethelbald. However, Aethelbald was murdered in 757 and Cynewulf seems to have been able to take advantage of the situation to claw back some land, as well as annexing some land belonging to the Hwicce, who were being absorbed into Mercia at the time (Yorke 1995 p62-63). Subsequently, Cynewulf granted land freely in Wiltshire. Only a charter of 758 was confirmed by Offa, and others give little or no sense that he was subservient to Mercia (Reynolds 2020 p 265). We also learned that he fought great battles against the Britons, which either did not worry the Mercians or they were powerless to stop him (*ASC* p47).

Reynolds deduces from this that Cynewulf had a reasonable amount of freedom, and that it would have been possible for Wessex to build East and West Wansdyke under his direction. It is likely that military service was a requirement of the landowning classes at this time, and this was the device used to organise a labour force for the project.

Reynolds and Langlands argue that what was conceived was a barrier all along the frontier between Wessex and Mercia, and they show how the two identifiable sections of West and East Wansdyke fit into this scheme.

From the west, they propose a line from Portishead running parallel to the River Avon, as proposed by Major and Burrow, ascending Dundry Hill from Yanley Lane, where we have already noted the charters of Edward II's reign, to Maes Knoll. There it follows the well attested line of West Wansdyke to Bath. The Roman Road between Bath and Morgan's Hill forms the next section, where it joins to East Wansdyke. The route continues through Savernake Forest and utilises the Bedwyn Dykes and the other short stretches of bank that have survived in this area, to reach Inkpen Beacon where the Counties of Wiltshire, Hampshire and Berkshire now meet (Reynolds and Langlands 2006 *passim*). Thereafter, it is argued, the frontier was on the line of the present boundary between Berkshire and Hampshire, though this section was never built. This is suspiciously straight save for a kink in the area of Silchester, which lies in Hampshire, severed from much of its surrounding territory. The line cuts through ecclesiastical and estate boundaries which were likely established before it was defined. It looks like an imposed line,

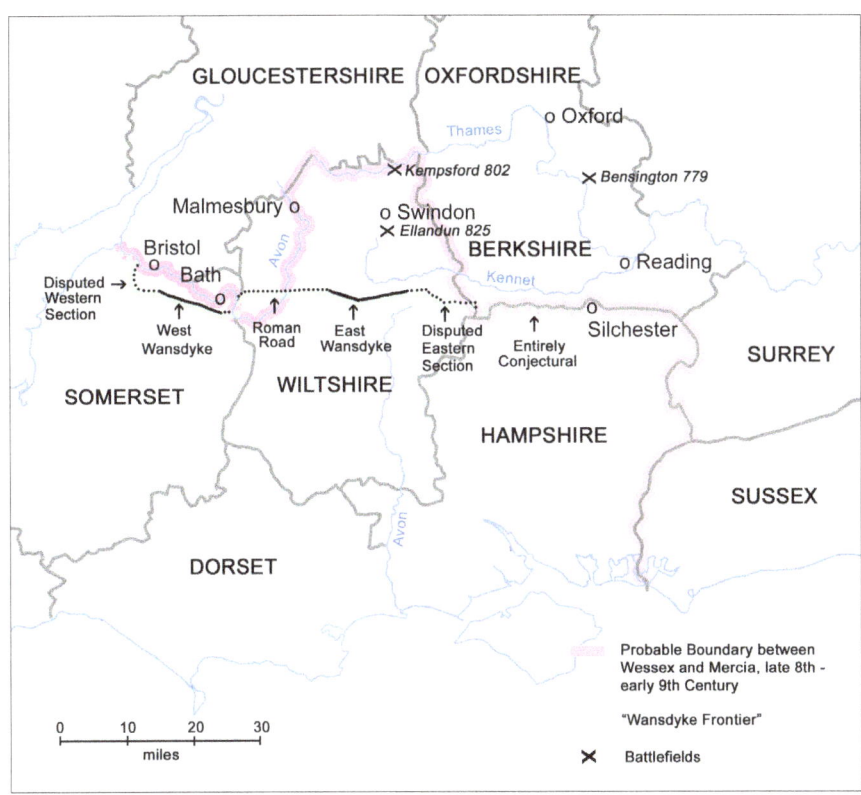

Reynolds and Langlands' proposed Wessex-Mercia boundary – A maximum view of Wansdyke

most likely during a period of Mercian dominance in the seventh or eighth centuries (Yorke 1995 p88, and see Eagles 2018 p176). This is argued to be the first of three successive, major frontiers demarcating the expansion of the Kingdom of Wessex, the others being, first, the River Thames and, second, the Danelaw Boundary imposed by Alfred the Great after the Battle of Ethendune in 878 (Reynolds and Langlands 2006 p 44).

The window within which Cynewulf could have created this frontier is considered to end with the Battle of Bensington in 779, where Cynewulf fought Offa and Offa 'took the settlement' (*ASC* 777(779)). The Abingdon Chronicle indicates that Offa now took control of Berkshire, Bath was taken back by Mercia and Cynewulf was obliged to sell land in Somerset to the Bishop of Worcester (Yorke 1995 p63). Wessex was subjugated to Mercia for the next 23 years until the Battle of Kempsford in 802 (Reynolds 2020 p 265).

It is from this scenario that we get the notion of Wansdyke as 'Wessex's equivalent of Offa's Dyke' (Reynolds 1999 p85). Indeed, assuming Offa's Dyke was actually built by Offa, then it must be at least possible that Wansdyke predates it, and that Offa got the idea from Cynewulf.

This scenario sits better with the argument that the dyke post-dates the parish boundaries that it crosses, as it is more likely that these boundaries would have been in place by this time. Reynolds and Langlands have also referred to David Hill's map of places visited by the kings of Wessex and Mercia up to 871 from his 1981 *Atlas of Anglo-Saxon England*. Those for Wessex are confined, with the exception of Chippenham, to locations south of Wansdyke, while those for Mercia are confined, again with one exception, to locations north of Wansdyke, a striking demonstration that this was the frontier between the two kingdoms (Hill 1981, Reynolds and Langlands 2006 pp 37-8).

As we saw in the last Chapter, it is unlikely that Wansdyke was built any later than the early years of the ninth century, indeed we can now say that it was unlikely to have been built later than 779, since between then and the Battle of Kempsford, Mercia would have kept close control of the border area. Then, with the battle of Kempsford the balance of power shifted, with Wessex gaining the upper hand into the ninth century.

And that is as far as we can take it at this point in time – the Hadrian's Wall or the Offa's Dyke of Wessex!

The Future

Wansdyke will remain an enigma until such time as it can be robustly dated. How this will happen is difficult to see at present. Consent to dig a scheduled ancient monument is very strictly controlled and difficult to obtain, and in any event, we have seen that the scarcity of finds from previous digs could liken this to looking for a needle in a haystack. Targetted excavation on the basis of geophysical survey would be absolutely essential, and we have seen in the case of the West Wansdyke excavations, where targetting was thoroughly undertaken, that the level of finds was still insufficient to provide that elusive dating evidence.

Radio carbon dating is also fraught with difficulties. First, few datable samples have been recovered as organic materials such as wood do not often survive from the date of original deposition. Second, where such materials are recovered it can be extremely difficult to be certain of their original context, which may have nothing to do with the excavation of the dyke.

Can the answer lie in the soil? Techniques are now available which can estimate when soil was last exposed to the atmosphere. Optically stimulated luminescence and archaeomagnetic dating have been suggested as a way forward for Wansdyke (Erskine 2008 p105, Bell 2012 pp104-5). OSL can measure the last time that a soil sample was exposed to sunlight by measuring trace amounts of isotopes of certain elements usually occurring in quartz or feldspar. Core samples could be taken at locations where it is known that the bank is in horizontal sections, such as Blackrock, Shepherd's Shore or Brown's Barn, where it may be hoped to pick up the dates of both stages of the earthwork's construction. Archaeomagnetic dating relies on the knowledge that the earth's magnetic field is constantly changing. When ferro-magnetic materials cool below the Curie Point (which happens when they are removed from a hearth for example) the electromagnetic signature is locked in the material. This can then be compared with other known signatures by measuring the declination of the magnetic field between that time and the present.

These techniques are improving and seem like the best way forward, but other techniques will almost certainly emerge in time. It seems likely that only then will the mystery that surrounds not only Wansdyke, but many other dykes, begin to be properly unravelled.

Visiting Wansdyke

It is to be hoped that readers who were not previously familiar with the earthwork will now want to explore it, while those that have visited it before may want to do so again with a new perspective.

East Wansdyke

Access to East Wansdyke, which is the best preserved section and so most rewarding to visit, is generally good. There is a dedicated Wansdyke Path which runs along the course of the dyke for most of its length. There is a short section around Red Shore where vegetation requires a small detour, but otherwise the route is continuous along the dyke from Morgans Hill to the Alton Barnes to Lockeridge road a mile east of Red Shore. Here a section of around a mile in the vicinity of Shaw House is not accessible before the footpath rejoins the earthwork shortly to the west of West Woods. From this point until it reaches the A345 the earthwork can be followed. East of the A345 the last mile and a half to New Buildings is not easy to access. A few paths cross the line of the dyke but none follows it.

There are four good parking spots. Smallgrain Plantation (SU020672), between Devizes and Calne, gives easy access to the western end of East Wansdyke and the junction of the dyke with the Roman road at Morgans Hill. From here, it is an easy walk down to Old Shepherd's Shore. A car park on the Alton Barnes - Lockeridge road near Adam's Grave (SU116637) is a good centre from which to explore Adam's Grave itself and the section of the dyke across the highest section of the Marlborough Downs from Red Shore to Tan Hill and beyond. Magnificent views are to be had both north to Silbury Hill and south across the Vale of Pewsey, and there is a real sense of being part of an ancient landscape.

Two further car parks give access to each end of West Woods. One is further up the Alton Barnes - Lockeridge road at SU134664 from which a track leads into the western side of the wood. The second is within the woods at SU163667 close to the dyke, access being obtained from a minor road running south from the A4 west of Marlborough to join the A345 a few miles south of the town. The Postern Hill car park at the north western corner of Savernake Forest (SU199679) is about a mile as the crow flies from New Buildings and gives access to the footpath network around the eastern end of the dyke, though, as noted above, exploring this end of the dyke is not straightforward and the results may be thought somewhat unrewarding.

West Wansdyke
Exploring West Wansdyke requires altogether more persistence and patience. Only two short sections of public footpath run along the line of the earthwork; one near its eastern end running west from a point opposite the Cross Keys pub on Midford Road, Bath, and the other on the north west flank of Stantonbury Hill. The latter is well worth the

NEAR HERE RUNS
WODEN'S DYKE
AN ANCIENT MONUMENT
AFTER WHICH
WANSDYKE COUNCIL
1974 - 1996
WAS NAMED

Footpath along West Wansdyke at Odd down, Bath

effort, however, as this is one of the best preserved sections of West Wansdyke.

In all other cases, it will be necessary to use paths which cross the dyke, and therefore afford views along it only. Views along the dyke are one of the best ways of appreciating it. A good view can be had from the

A367 (the Fosse Way) south of Bath. The view west shows Whistling Copse, Stantonbury and Maes Knoll closely aligned.

An approach to exploring West Wansdyke is to take a village as a base and explore it from the footpath network radiating out from it. Englishcombe, Stanton Prior and Compton Dando can each fulfill this role for their respective sections of the dyke, while a path leads up to Maes Knoll from Norton Malreward.

A Wansdyke Path

Robert Vermaat's Wansdyke21 website is also very helpful in giving directions to various sections of the earthwork as well as including many photographs. Vermaat's aim is to achieve a footpath along the length of the dyke from Maes Knoll to Savernake. As we have already noted, there is a good footpath serving East Wansdyke. Better access to West Wansdyke and the Roman road between Bath and Morgan's Hill could complete a splendid long distance pathway.

The aim of this book and the creation of a path running its whole length is to increase interest in Wansdyke. It is after all one of the biggest, yet least known, of Britain's ancient earth bank monuments. I hope that I have convinced readers that it deserves to be better known and better understood and to explore it for themselves.

Bibliography

Note: WAM is The Wiltshire Archaeological and Natural History Magazine

1. Ancient Texts

ASC: The Anglo-Saxon Chronicles translated and edited by Swanton, M, London 1996

Asser: Asser, *Life of King Alfred* translated by Keynes, S and Lapidge, M, London 1983

Bede: Bede, *The Ecclesiastical History of the English People* edited by McLure, J, and Collins, R, Oxford, 1994

Gallic Wars: Caesar, *The Gallic Wars* translated by McDevitte W A and Bohn W S at //classics.mit.edu/Caesar/gallic.html

Gildas: Gildas, *De Excidio Brittaniae (The Ruin of Britain)* edited and translated by Winterbottom, M, London 1978

Nennius: Nennius: *Historia Brittonum and The Welsh Annals* translated by Morris, J, London, 1980

Ptolemy : Ptolemy, *Geography,* www.roman-britain.org/ptolemys-geography.htm

Tacitus: Tacitus, *Annals* translated by Church A J and Brodripp W J at //classics.mit.edu/Tacitus/annals.html

2. Modern Texts

Aubrey 1675: Aubrey, J, *The Natural History of Wiltshire* first published by the Wiltshire Topographic Society in 1847, edited with notes by John Britton

Barrett 1789: Barrett, William, *The History and Antiquities of the City of Bristol,* place of publication unknown

Bell 2012: Bell, Mark, *The Archaeology of the Dykes* Stroud

Bettey 2003: Bettey, Joseph, *The First Historians of Bristol: William Barrett and Samuel Seyer,* Bristol

Bonney 1966: Bonney, D, 'Pagan Saxon Burials and Boundaries in Wiltshire' *WAM Vol 61*

Bonney 1972: Bonney, D, 'Early Boundaries in Wessex' in P Fowler (ed) *Archaeology and the Landscape* London

Brentnall 1924: Brentnall, H C, 'Wansdyke: The Savernake Section' *Report of the Marlborough College Natural History Society No 73*

Clark 1958: Clark, A, 'The Nature of Wansdyke', *Antiquity Vol 32*

Crawford 1953: Crawford, OGS, *Archaeology in the Field,* London

Crawford 1954: Crawford, OGS, 'The East End of Wansdyke', *WAM Vol 55* *(1953-4)*

Collinson 1792: Collinson, Rev John, *The History and Antiquities of the County of Somerset* (facsimile edition 1983) Stroud

Collingwood and Myres 1956: Collingwood, R and Myres, J, *Roman Britain and the English Settlements,* Oxford

Colt-Hoare 1819: Colt-Hoare, Sir Richard, *The Ancient History of North Wiltshire,* London

Colt-Hoare 1827: Colt-Hoare, Sir Richard, *Letter to the Philosophical and Literary Society at Bristol* https://archive.org/stream/ aletterstatingtoohoargoog#page/n11/mode/1up

Corney 2001: Corney, M, 'The Romano-British Nucleated Settlements of Wiltshire' in Ellis, P (ed) *Roman Wiltshire and After: Papers in Honour of Ken Annable,* Devizes

Costen 1987: Costen, M, 'Late Saxon Avon' in Aston, M, and Iles, R, (eds) *The Archaeology of Avon,* Bristol

Costen 2011: Costen, M. *Anglo-Saxon Somerset,* Oxford

Cunliffe 1993: Cunliffe, B, *Wessex to AD 1000,* London

Cunliffe 2005: Cunliffe, B, *Iron Age Communities in Britain, Fourth Edition,* London

Dark 1994: Dark, K, *Civitas to Kingdom,* London

Dark 2000; Dark, K, *Britain and the end of the Roman Empire,* Stroud

Dark 2001: Dark Age British Earthworks (interview with Robert Vermaat) at www.wansdyke21.org.uk/wansdyke/wanart/dark.htm

Devils Dyke Restoration Project at www.devilsdykeproject.org.uk

Draper 2006: Draper, S, *Landscape, Settlement and Society in Roman and early Medieval Wiltshire* Oxford

Eagles 2001: Eagles, B, 'Anglo-Saxon Presence and Culture in Wiltshire AD c.450-c.675' in Ellis, P (ed) *Roman Wiltshire and After: Papers in Honour of Ken Annable,* Devizes

Eagles 2018: Eagles, B. *From Roman Civitas to Anglo-Saxon Shire* Oxford

Eagles and Allen 2011: Eagles, B and Allen, M J 'A Reconsideration of East Wansdyke: Its Construction and Date - A Preliminary Note' in Brookes, S, Harrington, S and Reynolds, A *Studies in Early Anglo-Saxon Art and Archaeology: Papers in Honour of Martin G Welch (BAR British Series 527)* Oxford (republished in *Eagles 2018)*

Electronic Sawyer; at www.esawyer.org.uk

Erskine 2008: Erskine, J, 'The West Wansdyke: An Appraisal', *Archaeological Journal Vol 164,* London

Esmonde Cleary 2011: Esmonde Cleary, S, 'The Ending(s) of Roman Britain' in Hamerow, H et al (eds) *The Oxford Handbook of Anglo-Saxon Archaeology* Oxford

Fowler 2000: Fowler, P, *Landscape Plotted and Pieced,* Society of Antiquaries Research Report 64, London

Fowler 2001: Fowler, P, 'Wansdyke in the Woods' in Ellis, P (ed) *Roman Wiltshire and After: Papers in Honour of Ken Annable,* Devizes

Fox 2000: Fox, A, *Aileen - A Pioneering Archaeologist* Leominster

Fox and Fox 1960: Fox, A and Fox, Sir C, 'Wansdyke Reconsidered' *Archaeological Journal 115,* London

Gardner 1998: Gardner, K, 'The Wansdyke Diktat? A Discussion Paper' *Bristol and Avon Archaeology Vol 15* and at www.wansdyke21.org.uk/wansdyke/wanart/gardner1.htm

Guardian Obituary: www.guardian.co.uk/news/2006/jan/20/guardianobituaries.obituaries

Green 1971: Green, H S, 'Wansdyke, Excavations 1966 to 1970' *WAM Vol 67*

Grigg 2006: Grigg, E, 'Dark Age Dykes' at www.wansdyke21.org.uk/wansdyke/wanart/grigg.htm

Grundy 1919: Grundy, G B, 'The Saxon Land Charters of Wiltshire' (first series) *Archaeological Journal Vol 76*

Grundy 1920: Grundy, G B, 'The Saxon Land Charters of Wiltshire' (second series) *Archaeological Journal Vol 77*

Grundy 1939: Grundy, G B, 'The Ancient Woodland of Wiltshire' *WAM Vol 48*

Haslam 2011: Haslam, J, 'Daws Castle, Somerset, and Civil Defence Measures in Southern and Midland England in the Ninth to Eleventh Centuries' *Archaeological Journal Vol 168,* London

Higgins 2005: Higgins, David, *The History of The Bristol Region in The Roman Period,* Bristol

Higham 1992: Higham, N, *Rome, Britain and the Anglo-Saxons,* London

Hinton 2017: Hinton, David A: 'Wansdyke (East) Wiltshire – Notes for Visitors Prepared by the Royal Archaeological Institute' *RAI* ,London

Hirst et al. 1993: Hirst, S, Rahtz, P, Ashton, E, Bradley, R, Carter, H, Davies, J, Gardiner, J, Stevens, J, Taylor, R 'Liddington Castle and The Battle of Badon: Excavations and Research 1976' *Archaeological Journal Vol 153:1993* London

Hooke 1998: Hooke, D, *The Landscape of Anglo-Saxon England,* London

Hostetter and Howe 1997: Hostetter, E, and Howe, T N, 'Observations on the Bedwyn Dyke' in Hostetter, E and Howe, T N (eds) *The Romano-British Villa at Castle Copse, Great Bedwyn,* Bloomington, Indiana

Kirkham 2005: Kirkham, G, 'Prehistoric Linear Ditches on The Marlborough Downs' in Brown, G, Field, D and McOmish, D (eds) *The Avebury Landscape; Aspects of Field Archaeology of the Marlborough Downs* Oxford

Langlands 2019: Langlands, A, *The Ancient Ways of Wessex* Oxford

Laycock 2008: Laycock, S, *Britannia, The Failed State,* Stroud

Laycock 2009: Laycock, S, *Warlords,* Stroud

Leach 2001: Leach, P, *Roman Somerset,* Wimborne

Major 1913: Major, A , *Early Wars of Wessex,* Cambridge

Major 1924: Major, A, 'Excavations on Wansdyke' *WAM Vol 42*

Major and Burrow 1926: Major, A and Burrow, E, *The Mystery of Wansdyke,* Cheltenham

Malim 2020: Malim, T, 'Grimsditch, Wansdyke and The Ancient Highways of England' in *Offa's Dyke Journal Vol 2* Oxford

Matthews 2012: Matthews, R, *Ceawlin, The Man Who Created England* Barnsley

Moorhead 2001: Moorhead, T S N, 'Roman Coin Finds From Wiltshire' in Ellis, P (ed) *Roman Wiltshire and After: Papers in Honour of Ken Annable,* Devizes

Nurse 2002: Nurse, K, 'Late Roman Coin Hoards and Wansdyke' at www.wansdyke21.org.uk/wansdyke/wanart/nurse3.htm

Payne et al 2006: Payne, A, Corney, M and Cunliffe, B, *The Wessex Hillforts Project,* London, also at www.english-heritage.org.uk/publications/wessex-hillforts-project/

Pitt Rivers 1892: Pitt Rivers, Lt-Gen A H L-F *Excavations in Cranborne Chase, Vol III; Bokerly and Wansdyke,* Privately Printed

Rackham 2001: Rackham, O, *Trees & Woodland in the British Landscape* London

Reynolds 1999: Reynolds, A, *Later Anglo-Saxon England, Life and Landscape,* Stroud

Reynolds 2005: Reynolds, A 'From Pagus to Parish: Territory and Settlement in the Avebury Region from the Late Roman Period to the Domesday Survey' in Brown, G, Field, D and McOmish, D (eds) *The Avebury Landscape; Aspects of Field Archaeology of the Marlborough Downs* Oxford

Reynolds 2011: Reynolds, A, 'Crime and Punishment' in Hamerow, H et al (eds) *The Oxford Handbook of Anglo-Saxon Archaeology* Oxford

Reynolds 2020: Reynolds, A, 'A Possible Anglo-Saxon Execution Cemetery at Werg, Mildenhall (Cunetio), Wiltshire and The Wessex-Mercia Frontier in the Age of King Cynewulf' in *Offa's Dyke Journal Vol 2* Oxford

Reynolds and Langlands 2006: Reynolds, A and Langlands, A 'An Early Medieval Frontier: A Maximum View of Wansdyke' in Davies, W, (ed) *People and Space in Early Medieval Europe AD 300-1300* Turnhout

Rutter 1829: Rutter, J, *Delineations of the North Western Division of the County of Somerset,* Privately Published

Smith & Cox 1986: Smith, R. and Cox, P *The Past in The Pipeline – Archaeology of The Esso Midline,* Frome

Stukeley 1776: Stukeley, W, *Itinerarium Curiosum: Centura I,* London

Taylor 1904: Taylor, Rev C S, 'The Date of Wansdyke' *Transactions of the Bristol and Gloucestershire Archaeological Society, Vol 27* at www2.glos.ac.uk/bgas/tbgas/v027/bg027131.pdf

Vermaat 1999a: Vermaat, R, 'Wansdyke West to East' at www.wansdyke21.org.uk/wansdyke/wanwesteast/westeast.htm

Vermaat 1999b: Vermaat, R 'Forty Years of Fear' at www.vortigernstudies.org.uk/arthist/fortyyears.htm

Vermaat 2001: Vermaat, R, 'Wansdyke and the Roman Road' at www. wansdyke21.org.uk/wansdyke/wanart/road.htm

Wormald 1982: Wormald, P, 'The Ninth Century' in Campbell, J (ed)*The Anglo-Saxons* London

Yorke 1995: Yorke, B, *Wessex in the Early Middle Ages* London

Zaluskyj 2001: Zaluskyj, S, *Mercia, The Anglo-Saxon Kingdom of Central England* Logaston

Index

9 781914 407383